Merry Christmas

Cover illustrated by
Scott Gustafson

Cover text and border illustrated by
Stephanie Peterson

Treasury of Stories and Songs

PUBLICATIONS INTERNATIONAL, LTD.

Contents

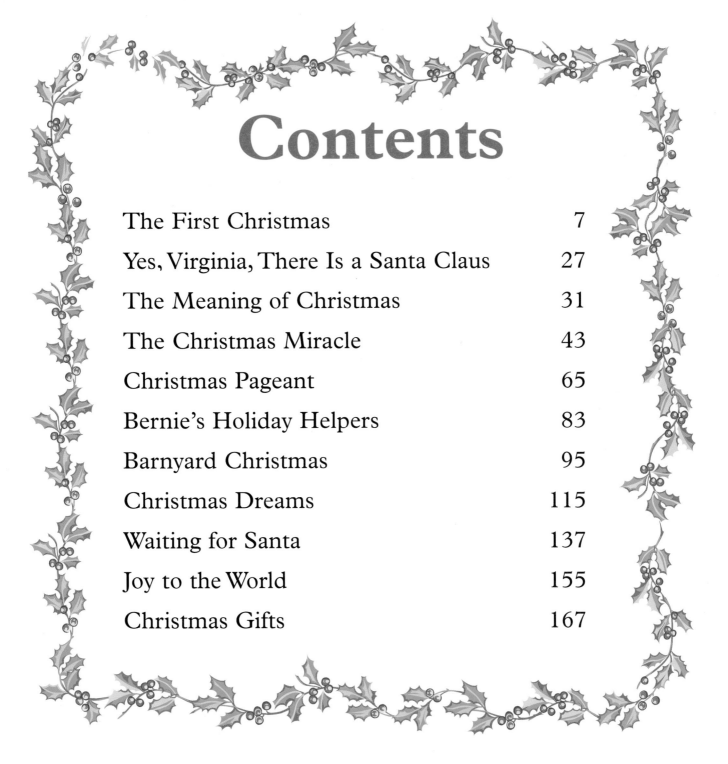

Contents

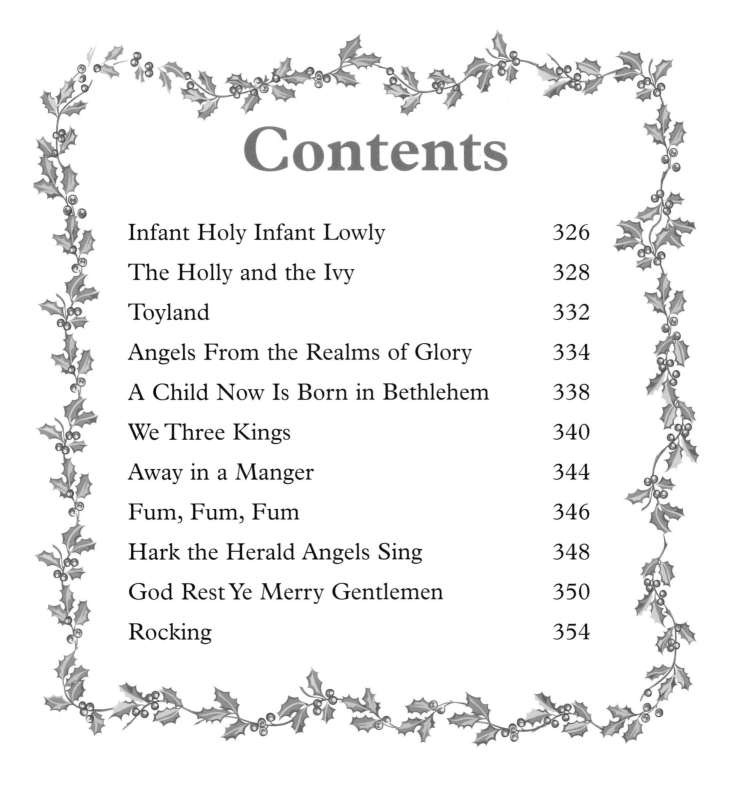

Contents

Contents

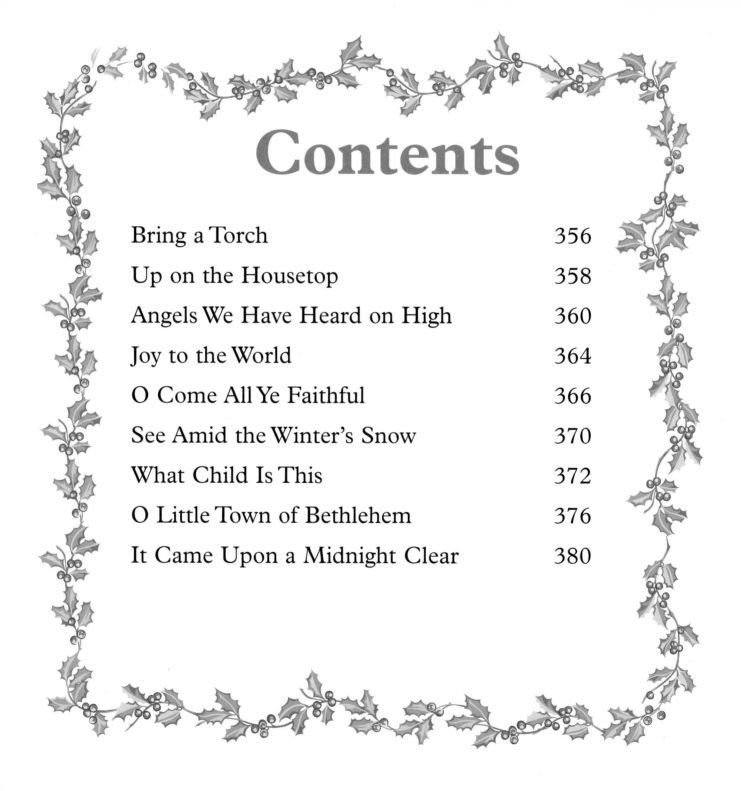

The First Christmas

Written by Sarah Toast

Illustrated by Michael Jaroszko

God had promised to send His Son to earth to be the world's Savior. When the time was right, God sent the angel Gabriel to Nazareth. There a young maiden named Mary lived. Mary was engaged to wed Joseph, a carpenter.

The angel appeared to Mary and said, "Rejoice! The Lord is with you. Do not be afraid, Mary. God has greatly blessed you. You are going to have a baby, and you will name Him Jesus. He will be the Son of God. His kingdom will never end."

Joseph was worried about Mary having a baby that was not his. Then the angel Gabriel appeared to Joseph in a dream. He told Joseph about Mary's Holy Child. Joseph understood. He wed Mary and took care of her.

Some months later, Rome's emperor announced that everyone in the land had to be counted. Men had to return to their hometown. There they would tell their name and what land they owned.

Joseph belonged to the family line of David. King David's birthplace was Bethlehem. So it was that Joseph left Nazareth, in Galilee, and set out for the distant town of Bethlehem, in Judea.

Joseph's young wife, Mary, went with him. She was nearing the time when she would give birth.

It was a long and difficult journey. Even though Mary rode the donkey while Joseph walked, she was weary. Her spirits lifted when they came to fields where sheep were grazing. Then the little town of Bethlehem came into view.

Night was falling when Joseph and Mary arrived in Bethlehem. Cattle were being led to the stables outside the town. The lamps were lit in the houses and inns.

Mary and Joseph knocked on the door of the first inn and waited. After what seemed like a long time, the innkeeper came to the door with his lantern.

The innkeeper told Joseph that he had no rooms left. Joseph and Mary tried several inns, but none had any room because so many people were staying in Bethlehem.

Finally one innkeeper noticed that Mary was heavy with child. The innkeeper told Joseph and Mary that they could spend the night in his stable with the animals.

That night in the stable, Mary gave birth to her baby, the Son of God. Mary wrapped the babe in light swaddling cloths and laid Him in a manger. Mary and Joseph named the baby Jesus.

The manger was filled with soft, clean hay, intended to feed the cattle. This was the first bed for the infant Jesus.

Mary rested near the manger while her newborn son slept peacefully. Joseph sat quietly beside her. The gentle animals in the stable crowded near the infant. Their sweet breath warmed the family.

Outside in the night sky, a bright new star appeared in the east. This was a very special star and it shone like no other star in the sky. It has come to be known as the Star of Bethlehem.

In the fields outside the town, shepherds were keeping watch over their sheep through the night.

Suddenly there was a great light, and an angel of the Lord appeared before them. The shepherds were very much afraid.

The angel spoke to the shepherds, saying, "Fear not, for I bring you wonderful news. It will bring great joy to all the world. For there is born to you this night in Bethlehem a Savior, who is Christ the Lord. And this is how you will know Him: You will find a baby wrapped in swaddling cloths, lying in a manger."

Then all at once many angels appeared in the sky.

The angels sang praises: "Glory to God in the highest, and on earth peace and goodwill toward all people."

The shepherds said to one another, "Let us go to this baby that God's angels have told us about."

The shepherds hurried to Bethlehem through the bright, starlit night. Soon they found Mary and Joseph resting in the stable, and the baby Jesus wrapped in swaddling cloths asleep in the manger.

Back at their fields, they told everyone that they had seen the Savior. All who heard were amazed!

In a land far to the east, there lived three Wise Men, Gaspar, Melchior, and Balthasar.

On the night of Jesus' birth, these Wise Men saw a bright new star in the heavens. They knew the star was a sign that the Savior had been born. They learned that Bethlehem was the birthplace.

They decided they must go worship the newborn King. They gathered gifts of gold, frankincense, and myrrh and set off on their long journey.

The three Wise Men traveled the long road to Bethlehem by camel caravan with their gifts for the baby Jesus. To their great joy and wonder, the same bright star that they had seen first in the east went ahead of them. Its light guided them on their long journey. The star's ever-present glow led them over the hills and across valleys.

The Wise Men followed the star westward until they reached Bethlehem. Then the Star of Bethlehem seemed to stand still. It streamed its light down on a small stable. The Wise Men knew that this must be where the infant Jesus lay. They approached the stable.

It had been a long journey, but the Wise Men had finally reached their destination. They came to the place the star was shining on. Inside the stable, they saw the baby with His mother, Mary. Gazing on the child, the Wise Men fell to their knees and worshiped the infant.

Then they opened the treasures they had brought from the east. They presented the infant Jesus with the rare gifts of gold, frankincense, and myrrh.

Soon others came from all over the land to worship the newborn Son of God. They knew that He was a very wonderful child and that the day He was born would always be remembered as a very special day throughout time.

Mary looked lovingly at her child. She thought about how the Lord had blessed her. In her heart, she praised the Lord, and her spirit rejoiced.

From then on, the day that baby Jesus was born would be known as Christmas Day and the world would celebrate!

Yes, Virginia, There Is a Santa Claus

Illustrated by Wayne Parmenter

In 1897, eight-year-old Virginia O'Hanlon asked the question, "Is there a Santa Claus?" She wrote a letter to the editor of *The New York Sun* requesting an honest reply.

This is what her letter said:

Dear Editor:

I am eight years old. Some of my little friends say there is no Santa Claus. Papa says, "If you see it in The Sun it's so."

Please tell me the truth, is there a Santa Claus?

Virginia O'Hanlon
115 West 95th Street

An editor for *The Sun*, Francis P. Church, received little Virginia's letter and wrote the following reply. It was printed in the September 21, 1897 edition of *The New York Sun*.

Virginia, your little friends are wrong. They have been affected by the skepticism of a skeptical age. They do not believe except they see. They think that nothing can be which is not comprehensible by their little minds. All minds, Virginia, whether they be men's or children's, are little. In this great universe of ours man is a mere insect, an ant, in his intellect, as compared with the boundless world about him, as measured by the intelligence capable of grasping the whole of truth and knowledge.

Yes, Virginia, there is a Santa Claus. He exists as certainly as love and generosity and devotion exist, and you know that they abound and give to your life its highest beauty and joy. Alas, how dreary would be the world if there were no Santa Claus! It would be as dreary as if there were no Virginias.

There would be no childlike faith then, no poetry, no romance to make tolerable this existence. We should have no enjoyment, except in sense and sight. The eternal light with which childhood fills the world would be extinguished.

Not believe in Santa Claus! You might as well not believe in fairies! You might get your papa to hire men to watch in all the chimneys on Christmas Eve to catch Santa Claus coming down, but what would that prove? Nobody sees Santa Claus.

The most real things in the world are those that neither children nor men can see. Did you ever see fairies dancing on the lawn? Of course not, but that's no proof that they are not there. Nobody can conceive or imagine all of the wonders there are unseen and unseeable in the world.

You tear apart a baby's rattle and see what makes the noise inside, but there is a veil covering the unseen world which not the strongest man, nor the united strength of all the strongest men that ever lived, could tear apart. Only faith, fancy, poetry, love, romance can push aside that curtain and view and picture the supernal beauty and glory beyond. Is it all real? Ah, Virginia, in this world there is nothing else real and abiding.

No Santa Claus! Thank God he lives, and lives forever. A thousand years from now, Virginia, nay ten times ten thousand years from now, he will continue to make glad the heart of childhood.

The Meaning of Christmas

Written by Lisa Harkrader

Illustrated by Deborah Colvin Borgo

Santa looked at the line of children waiting to see him. "Christmas means so much to the kids," he said.

One by one the children sat on Santa's lap. One by one they told Santa what they wanted for Christmas. Each child had a longer list than the child before. Santa listened as the children asked for more and more and bigger and bigger presents.

"Oh, dear!" thought Santa. "Have I been too busy making lists and building toys? Did I let the kids forget the true meaning of Christmas?"

Santa began asking each child, "What do you think Christmas is about?"

"Presents, of course," said Jeff.

"Vacation from school," said Amanda.

"Cookies," said Ross, "with frosting."

Nate was last in line. He scrambled onto Santa's lap. Santa looked at the long, long list that Nate had in his hand and sighed.

Nate smoothed out his list and began reading.

"First of all," said Nate, "I need garden tools. And there's a very good reason why."

Santa barely listened to Nate as he read his list. He was too sad and too worried. He was sad the kids didn't remember the meaning of Christmas. He was worried that he had been too busy to help them remember. He heard Nate say something about a music box, a barbecue grill, and dog biscuits.

Santa sat up straight. "Dog biscuits?"

"Yes," said Nate. "The flavored kind."

Santa shook his head. "If that's what you want." He gave Nate a candy cane and sent him on his way. He didn't ask Nate what he thought Christmas really meant.

Christmas Eve arrived, and Santa was running late. His bag was so heavy it bogged down the sleigh. It was so bulky Santa could barely get it down the chimneys.

"It's the toys," Santa told Blitzen. "There are more toys this year than ever before."

By the time Santa reached Nate's house, it was almost midnight. Nate was already fast asleep.

"It's almost Christmas Day," Santa told Blitzen, "and I haven't found anybody who knows what Christmas is all about."

The sleigh landed on Nate's roof. Santa checked to make sure all of Nate's gifts were in his bag. "Nate asked for some peculiar gifts this year," he said. "Garden tools, a music box, a barbecue grill, and dog biscuits."

Santa heaved his bulging bag over his shoulder. "I've really let the kids down," he told Blitzen. "They think Christmas is what I carry in this bag. It's all my fault."

Blitzen snorted and stamped his hoof on the snow-covered roof.

"Snort all you like. It's true," Santa said.

"Wish me luck," Santa said. "You know what happened at the Murphy house."

Santa grabbed his bag firmly, climbed into the chimney, and slid down. Halfway to the bottom, Santa's bulging bag skidded to a stop. Santa and the toys were stuck.

"Oh, dear," said Santa. "I was afraid of this."

Santa tugged on the bag. It slid free. Santa landed with a thud in the fireplace.

"Just like the Murphy house," he mumbled.

Santa set about his business, leaving gifts for Nate and his family. He pulled the first gift from his bag.

"I can't imagine what Nate wants with garden tools. Still, it's what he asked for." Santa consulted his list. "Oh, my." Santa blinked. "Nate doesn't want these tools for himself. They're for his mother."

Santa scratched his head. He thought back to the day Nate had come to sit on his lap. He tried to remember what Nate had said. "Nate told me his mother loves her garden, but her old tools are rusty. Ho-ho-ho! I should've paid closer attention."

Santa studied his list even closer.

"The music box is for his sister, and the barbecue grill is for his dad. Nate wanted to make sure his family got exactly what they wanted. He even remembered dog biscuits for his dog. Well, I won't let them down."

Santa bounded about the room, leaving gifts and filling stockings. When he reached Nate's stocking, he found something already inside. It was a small wrapped package. The tag said, "To Santa."

Santa opened the gift. It was a pair of earmuffs. Underneath was a note:

Dear Santa,

    You forgot to ask me what Christmas is all about. Jeff said Christmas is about presents, and he's right. I make my family happy when I give them a gift that they really want.

Amanda said Christmas is about vacation, and she's right, too. During Christmas break my family has time to decorate our tree and bake cookies. That means Ross was right, too. Christmas is about cookies.

But mostly I think Christmas is about believing in things you love, even when they're hard to see. Like you.

Love,

Nate

P.S. I hope you like the earmuffs. I don't want you to get sick. Christmas wouldn't be Christmas without you.

Santa read the letter twice. "Nate's right," he said. "Christmas is about believing in the things you love. The kids didn't forget that, but I did. I stopped believing in the kids."

As Santa turned to leave, he saw the mantel clock. Midnight had passed. It was now officially Christmas Day.

"Well, it's Christmas and I finally found somebody who remembers the true meaning of Christmas," Santa said, donning his earmuffs. "Little Nate and me, too."

Santa patted his new earmuffs and put a little extra something in Nate's stocking. It turned out that he didn't let the children down after all.

The Christmas Miracle

Written by Pegeen Hopkins

Illustrated by Linda Graves

Once upon a time there lived a poor Dutch baker. He never had enough money to buy food. Each winter, the baker's problems got worse. When the temperature fell, people stayed home and didn't buy bread.

One December night, the wind was blowing strong and not a single person had come in that day. "What will I do?" the baker muttered. It was getting late, so he locked the bakery door. Then he started home.

Every day the baker skated along an icy canal to get to the bakery. "I will carry the leftover bread home to my wife," he thought. "It will have to be enough for us to eat."

He walked slowly to the frozen canal — with his teeth chattering the whole way. When he got there, he saw the local farmer passing by.

The farmer had had a bad day at the market, too. He had hoped to sell the apples from his tiny orchard. But by the end of the day he had sold only ten. He had to bring his sackful of apples home so they wouldn't go bad in the frost. This made him sad. He needed guilders, small Dutch coins, to buy medicine for his daughter who was very sick.

The baker and the farmer were the only two men on the ice. They fell into step naturally and skated together down the canal.

Before long, another man showed up. As he
skated toward the baker and the farmer, he
thought about the long day he had had.

The new skater was a talented weaver on his
way home from the marketplace, too. He made
warm blankets and pretty coats. But no one
could buy the weaver's goods. They cost too
much. Most people in the small Dutch town
made do with what they had. They rarely
bought things new.

The weaver had wanted to make enough to
buy his old father the lemon tea he liked so
much. But all the weaver had was blankets.
Like the other two men, he had no money.

Because he wanted company, the weaver joined the baker and the farmer.

A cold, sharp wind ripped at the men as they skated. So they lowered their heads to protect themselves from the cold. They listened to the wind blowing through the trees on the side of the canal. The whining of the wind seemed to get louder and louder. It became so strong that it sounded like a baby crying.

The farmer saw an old, deserted stable in the distance. He had fond memories of playing there when he was a boy. But that was many years ago. Now the stable was in ruins.

The farmer realized that the crying sound was not the wind. It was coming from inside the stable. "That can't be," he thought out loud. "No one has been in that stable for years."

"Do you think the crying is coming from over there?" asked the baker. He had been thinking the very same thing as the farmer.

"Let's go see," said the weaver. The weaver led the baker and the farmer across the ice and up the hill to the stable.

When they reached the door, the men looked inside. They could not believe their eyes. A young woman sat on the floor, holding a baby boy in her arms.

It had been the baby making the noise, not the wind. A man sat next to them on a crate. He held his head in his hands, looking very sad.

"What are you doing here?" asked the baker. "This is no place for a family. It is much too cold. You can't stay here."

"We are traveling through Amsterdam on our way to visit relatives," the man replied. "It got so cold and dark we had to find shelter."

The farmer turned to look at the young woman and the baby, who was now fast asleep.

"What will you eat?" the farmer asked. When he looked at the peaceful boy, he immediately thought of his sick daughter at home.

"We have nothing," replied the young man.

"Here," the baker exclaimed suddenly, "take this bread. It's not much. But you need it more than I do."

One by one, the men took their sacks and emptied them in front of the woman and child. They stacked the bread, apples, and blankets in neat piles on the floor. The family looked at the men in awe.

"My prayers have been answered," cried the woman. "Our son was so hungry and cold. We will not forget your kindness. But we can never repay you," she explained. "We are very poor."

"We understand," replied the men.

During the short time the men were in the stable, the wind had died down. A light snow began to fall. Each man had a warm feeling inside. Their thoughts and their bags did not weigh them down any more. They skated together like good friends.

"Maybe our luck will be better tomorrow at the marketplace," said the baker. But the men's luck would change sooner than tomorrow.

As they skated toward home, the men felt the sacks on their backs getting heavier, as if they were filling up.

"The snow must be falling hard," each man thought. "I can feel it falling in my bag."

When the baker reached his house and left the others, they saw that his bag was fat and bulging. "Merry Christmas," he said to his new friends. The farmer and the weaver waved back at him as he walked toward his house.

Then the baker removed his skates and trudged through the heavy snow. When he arrived home, he opened his front door. Only then did he see that his bag was bulging — but not with snow, as he had thought. The bag was bursting with gold coins and food of all sorts! There was even a silk scarf for his wife and toys for the children.

"My, the market must have been very busy today," said the baker's wife. "How can we afford all of these wonderful gifts?"

The baker could not explain the wonderful gifts. He just shook his head and said, "I guess we deserve them, dear."

At that moment, the baker knew that when his friends got home they would find their bags filled with gifts, too.

And they did. When the farmer reached his house, he turned to the weaver and said, "I hope we will meet on the canal again."

"Merry Christmas," said the weaver.

Then the farmer went into his house.

Then he realized why his bag felt so full. It held many guilders and enough medicine to cure his daughter!

The weaver found the same fortune upon his return home. His bag was full of the lemon tea his father loved so much!

For their kindness, the baker, the weaver, and the farmer had found more than good luck. They had found a miracle.

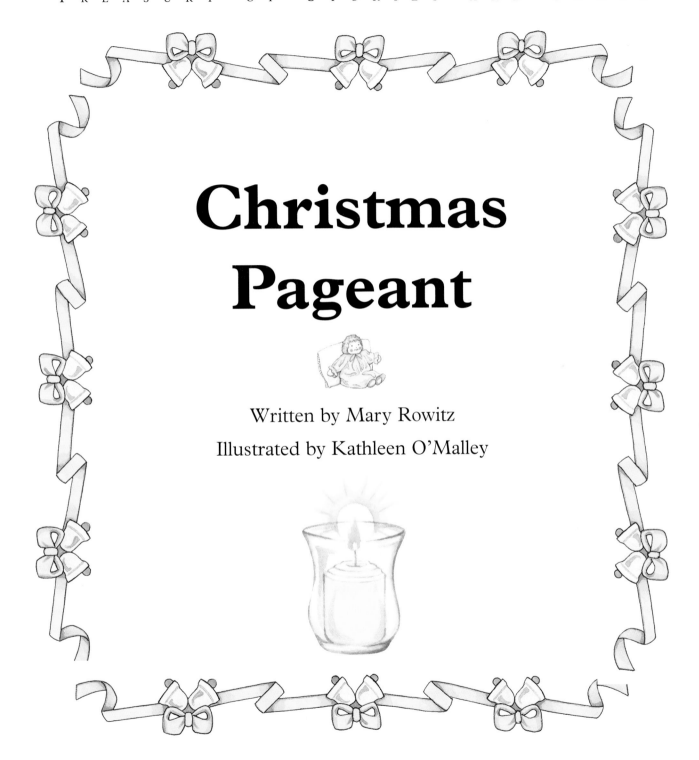

Christmas Pageant

Written by Mary Rowitz

Illustrated by Kathleen O'Malley

It is the night of the Christmas pageant. Children are ready to play the parts of Mary, Joseph, the shepherds, and the three Wise Men. They will tell the story of the birth of Jesus.

Jimmy, who plays a shepherd, grips his father's hand tightly.

"Jimmy, if you forget what you are supposed to say, think about the meaning of the story," Jimmy's father says. "That should help you remember."

Jimmy watches his friends Greg and Sarah, who play Joseph and Mary, go on stage. At rehearsals, Greg and Sarah had always giggled when they said their lines. But now, they both look serious.

On stage, Greg notices that the boy playing the innkeeper has buttoned up his shirt wrong! Greg thinks this is very funny. But he clears his throat and says his lines, without even a tiny giggle.

Off stage, Greg and Sarah burst out laughing. Jimmy giggles, too.

Now it's Jimmy's turn on stage. He walks out from behind the curtain. There are so many faces in the audience!

Jimmy bends down to feed a lamb, but can't remember his lines! He thinks about the meaning of the story, like his father told him. He takes a deep breath.

"Christ the Savior is born today," Jimmy says. "Let's praise the Baby Jesus."

Jimmy looks at the audience. The faces are all smiling! He smiles, bows and looks around for his father. His father gives him a wink.

Jimmy stands backstage, bouncing with excitement. His friend Tina takes the stage as she sings a Christmas song.

With a big smile, blue eyes, and blonde, curly hair Tina looks exactly like an angel should, Jimmy thinks.

As Tina steps across the stage, her right shoe slips off and lands at the edge of the stage! But she keeps singing. Tina takes off her other shoe and sits down.

Jimmy looks at Tina on stage and thinks that angels should not wear shoes, anyway.

It's time for Jimmy's next scene. When Rob, the other shepherd, joins him on stage, Jimmy sees that he is very nervous. Jimmy remembers his father and winks at Rob. He says, "Just do what I do, and you'll be fine."

Rob smiles at his friend.

Jimmy kneels. So does Rob.

Jimmy bows his head. So does Rob.

"Baby Jesus," Jimmy says, "you will have many special friends in your life."

Rob is thankful Jimmy is his friend.

As Jimmy walks off stage, the three Wise Men, played by Matt, Andy, and Sean, are walking on. Jimmy had helped them pick out gifts for the Baby Jesus.

First comes Matt, who brought some of his best rocks from his collection. He carries them in a colorful box.

Next comes Andy, who put his favorite jelly beans in a jar. He ate a few backstage, but there are still plenty left.

Last comes Sean, who brought his pet mouse. He just hopes no one opens the box on stage!

Now Jimmy and the other children gather on stage. A bright spotlight shines on the baby. The three Wise Men offer their gifts to little Jesus.

Jimmy and Rob are no longer so nervous but think about how shepherds behave. John and Sarah no longer feel like giggling. Sean forgets about his pet mouse in his box.

The children close their eyes and pretend that they are in Bethlehem on the day Jesus is born. They bow their heads and pray to the Baby Jesus.

Jimmy watches as Sarah, who plays the part of Mary, holds the Baby Jesus. He hopes she doesn't giggle during this last scene.

Jimmy has nothing to worry about. Sarah looks at the baby and speaks just as a mother would.

"I love you very much," she says. "You are my special baby. As you grow up, I want you to laugh and have fun. But just remember that there are times to be serious, too."

Everyone thinks Sarah has chosen the perfect words to say.

Sarah, Jimmy, and the rest of the children have managed to capture the true meaning of Christmas with their play. Their performance has made this the most wonderful Christmas pageant the town has ever seen!

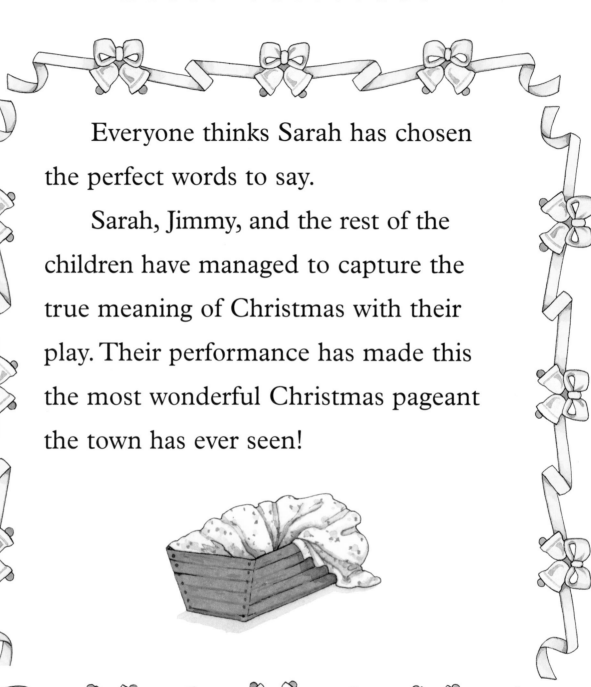

Bernie's Holiday Helpers

Written by Pegeen Hopkins

Illustrated by Linda Howard

Every Christmas, Bernie Bear and his family travel to visit Aunt Betty. The trip is always exciting for young Bernie. Everyone helps load presents into the Bear family's big red sled. Then they are off on their trip, singing and laughing as they travel.

But this year will be different. "The bad news is that we have to wait at the den for Cousin Barney. He won't be here until the day before Christmas," says Father Bear.

Mother Bear continues, "But we know that you are a responsible bear, so we are letting you go to Aunt Betty's ahead of us, by yourself!"

"You mean it?" asks Bernie. "Can I take the sled, too?"

"Of course," they reply. "You can bring your friend Freddie Fox. Aunt Betty loves company. 'The more the merrier' is her motto."

When the morning of the trip arrives, the two friends start on their way.

As Bernie guides the sled across the snow, just one thing bothers him. He is a little bit nervous. It is, after all, his first trip without his parents. Then Bernie's face brightens. He knows everything will work out.

Before they go far, they pass a hollow oak tree where Ralph Raccoon lives.

Ralph Raccoon has great vision in the dark, much better than either Bernie or Freddie.

"I have an idea," says Bernie. "Let's ask Ralph to come to Aunt Betty's. We got a late start and the sun may go down before we even arrive there."

Bernie explains his plan to Ralph Raccoon. Ralph is happy to come along.

"Count me in," says Ralph. "I'd be glad to help you get to Aunt Betty's. I love when she makes that tuna nutmeg pie!"

"Oh, she's already baking," says Bernie.

Very soon, the three travelers are merrily on their way.

Soon they approach Rhonda Rabbit's house. Bernie has another great idea! "All this snow may cover the ice on the lake. We won't know exactly where the ice is," Bernie says. "It's best for us to stay on firm ground. If Rhonda joins us, she can burrow through the snow if it gets too deep and check our path so we stay safe."

It is a fact that Rhonda can burrow faster and farther than anyone in town. Every summer at the Bearville Carnival, Rhonda wins the "Burrow Bonanza." All the best burrowers show up to compete for the top prize—a year's supply of carrots!

When they get to Rhonda's, Bernie finds it easy to convince her to join them. She hops into the sled and begins singing sledding songs as they cross the snowy landscape.

Bernie smiles as he looks around the sled. He is thinking about what a good time they are having. It is fun to have a lot of friends along!

Then Bernie has another idea! "I'm going to stop by Oliver Owl's," he says. "Oliver can fly on ahead and check the roads. Last year, we had to travel miles out of our way because a pine tree had fallen on our path. If we had known, we could have tried another route."

Oliver flies from his perch high in the trees as soon as he hears the sleigh bells on the sled. He hopes the crowd will invite him along. When they do, Oliver is pleased to join them.

The happy band continues on its way. By now, the sled is filled with more animals than usual. Their weight pushes the sled deeper into the snow, slowing them down. But, Bernie is pleased with their pace. He likes spending time with his friends.

Bernie is concerned, though, that he cannot steer the sled very well anymore. Ice on the bottom of the sled is making it hard to handle. He knows he should take care of this, but how will he do it? Then Bernie gets another idea!

"I know!" Bernie nearly shouts. "Charlie Chipmunk has small hands. He could fit them under the sled and wipe off all the ice. I wonder if he wants to come, too?"

When the sled comes to his underground hole, Charlie pops out and scampers over. Bernie quickly explains the problem.

It turns out that Charlie has no plans for the holiday. "This will be fun," Charlie says. "Of course I'll come along!" Before he jumps in, Charlie bends down and sticks his tiny paws under the sled. Soon every icicle and clump of snow is gone.

When Charlie is finished, Bernie yells, "Next stop, Aunt Betty's…full speed ahead!"

With that, they take off into the woods for the final part of the trip. Bernie isn't worried about anything anymore. His parents knew he would be able to figure everything out, and he is having a great adventure traveling with his friends. Besides, they make such a great team that Bernie wonders where they will all go for the next holiday!

Barnyard Christmas

Written by Lisa Harkrader

Illustrated by Laura Rader

On Christmas Eve, all the farm animals gathered in the barnyard. They watched the farm family decorate the farmhouse. Cow strained her neck over the fence so she wouldn't miss anything. Pig crowded in beside her.

"What in blazes are they doing?" asked Old Crow as he watched the farm family, too.

Goat replied, "Tying bows on the lamppost and dragging trees indoors."

"Isn't it lovely?" said Cow.

"Lovely?" squawked Rooster. "It's absurd. And who is this red-nosed reindeer they keep singing about?"

"Foolishness!" said Goat. "Plain foolishness!"

"It's not foolish," said Cow. "It's wonderful. I only wish we could be part of it," she sighed. "They've forgotten us again."

Cow took one last look at the farmhouse, then plodded into the barn.

"Now we've done it," said Pig.

"Cow has no business moping about," said Rooster. "Didn't the farmer give her a woolly scarf? Nobody else in the barn got a gift."

"A gift!" said Pig. "That's it! If Cow can't be part of Christmas at the farmhouse, we'll bring part of Christmas to the barn. And I know the part Cow loves best—the Christmas tree."

"You can't cut down a tree and drag it into the barnyard," said Rooster.

"No," said Pig. "I can't." He hung his head.

Then Pig perked up. "But I can make the shape of a tree. Out of snow."

"Nonsense!" said Goat.

Pig rolled a big snowball and then a small snowball. Mare placed one on top of the other.

"Big on the bottom. Little at the top," said Pig to Mare.

"Just like a tree," said Mare.

"Needs branches," said Goat.

Pig looked at the tree. Then Mare looked at the tree. "I'm afraid he's right," said Mare.

"Well, we can't make branches out of snow," said Pig. "Where will we get the branches for our Christmas tree?"

"Foolishness!" said Goat. He ambled over to the brush pile and came back with two sticks. He stuck one stick on each side of the snow tree.

"Perfect!" said Pig to Goat.

"Just the thing!" added Mare.

"Now we decorate," said Pig. "Cow says the farm family starts with candy canes."

"Fascinating!" said Rooster. "But I haven't noticed many candy canes lying about the barn lately. Have you?"

Pig shook his head. "Maybe we can find something that looks like a candy cane. Something long and skinny."

The smallest rabbit stood up on his hind legs. "We have just the thing," he said.

The rabbits hopped to their hole and returned with a carrot.

"This is just the thing," said Pig. He stretched up and poked it into the snow tree.

Pig looked at the tree again. "It's still a little bare," he said.

"In my experience," Rooster said, "Christmas trees always have something bright on top, like a star. It's a signal for that flying Ho-Ho-Ho fellow who comes every year."

"Bright? Did you say bright?" asked Old Crow as he hopped down from the fence. "If bright is what you need, I have just the thing for your Christmas tree."

Old Crow flew into the cornfield and took the striped cap from the scarecrow's head. He circled back to the barnyard and dropped the cap on the very top of the snow tree.

"This is very bright indeed!" said Pig.

"And colorful, too!" added Mare.

The cap gave Pig an idea.

"I know what we need," said Pig. "Socks!"

"Socks?" said Rooster. "Whatever for?"

"The farm family hangs socks on the mantel," said Pig. "Mr. Ho-Ho-Ho puts toys in them."

Mama Cat stood and stretched. "My children may have just the thing," she said. Her kittens ran into the barn and returned with mittens.

"These are just the thing," said Pig.

"I don't suppose anyone has noticed that we don't have a fireplace," said Rooster.

"No," said Pig.

"You're right. We don't," said Mare.

"Let's use the branches on the tree," said
Goat. And so they did.

Mare took the mittens and
hung one on the end of
each branch.

"Are we finished?" asked Rooster.

Pig studied the snow tree. "We've forgotten something," he said. "Twinkly lights."

"No," clucked Rooster. "The barnyard will look like a carnival."

"But Cow loves twinkly lights," said Pig.

"Doesn't matter," said Goat. "We don't have lights anyway, twinkly or otherwise."

"We have something," squeaked a tiny voice.

The animals looked down. Three field mice ran into the barn and returned with two shiny buttons.

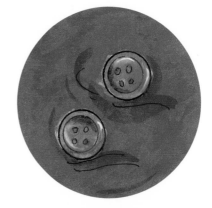

"Perfect!" said Pig.

"Now we need ornaments,"
said Pig.

"Ornaments?" asked Mare.

"What do they look like?" asked Rooster.

"Shiny, dangly, and mostly roundish," said Pig.

Rooster flapped his wings. "I know just the thing. Broken egg shells from the last bunch of chicks that hatched."

"Not dangly enough," said Goat.

"Really?" squawked Rooster. "And what would you suggest? More sticks?"

While Rooster and Goat argued, the squirrels scurried up to their nest. They returned with three large acorns.

Goat stopped. Rooster blinked. Pig stared.

"Acorns!" said Pig.

Pig placed the acorns in a neat row on the snow tree. He stood back to admire his work. "We need one last thing," Pig said. "The farm family wraps long strings of popcorn around their tree."

"Splendid!" said Rooster. "But we don't seem to have a popcorn popper handy."

"We could find something similar," said Pig. The barn swallow flew into the barn and returned a moment later with Cow's woolly scarf. She draped it around the snow tree, just in time.

Suddenly, Cow marched out of the barn.

"Merry Christmas!" shouted the animals.

Cow stopped. She looked at the tree.

"A snowman!" said Cow excitedly.

"A snowman?" asked Pig.

Pig hung his head. "We wanted to give you part of Christmas. We thought we were making a Christmas tree."

"If you wanted to give me part of Christmas," Cow said, "this snowman is just the thing. Merry Christmas, everyone!"

Christmas Dreams

Written by Suzanne Lieurance

Illustrated by Michael Carroll

It's Christmas Eve. Everyone is busy, everyone but Freddie.

"I'm bored," says Freddie.

"Well," says Mom, "use your imagination."

"A lot of good that will do," he says. Just then, Freddie hears a knock at the door. He opens the door, but no one is there. He looks down to find a shiny package with his name on it and a card.

"What's this?" he wonders. "The card says, 'Do not open until Christmas morning.'"

Freddie is still thinking about what could be in the package as he climbs into bed.

Soon he is dreaming. "Who are you?" he asks some scary monsters who appear in his dreams.

"Just your imagination," they answer.

"Hmm," says Freddie. "Monsters are boring. All they do is try to scare people. I'm not scared of you. I think I'll imagine something else."

"Ahoy, matey. Come aboard and help us find the treasure," says a voice.

"Pirates!" says Freddie. "Buried treasure!"

Freddie and his imaginary pirates set sail to a small island looking for treasure.

"X marks the spot," says one of the pirates as he looks at a big treasure map.

The pirates begin digging and digging. Finally, they find a treasure chest filled with gold doubloons.

"Wow! Look at all the gold!" says Freddie. "Who would have imagined that?"

"Why, you just did," say the pirates.

"Oh, yeah," says Freddie. "My imagination. I guess I'll use it to find a new place to hide this treasure. Ready for takeoff! Blast off!"

Freddie heads for the moon in his very own rocket ship. The houses below him get farther and farther away. Freddie waves to the man in the moon.

"I'm coming to see you and hide this treasure," Freddie says to the man in the moon.

"Your very own rocket," says the moon. "Well, imagine that."

"I just did," says Freddie. "Haven't you heard? I have a remarkable imagination."

Just then, Freddie feels his tummy start to rumble.

"I must be getting hungry," says Freddie. "But I'm not in the mood for any green cheese!"

Freddie's tummy rumbles again. "I'll just imagine something to eat."

Since Freddie has such a remarkable imagination, a giant, fancy machine appears. It's something to behold! It mixes and measures, stirs and pours, making the best desserts anyone has ever imagined.

Klunk! Bang! Boom! Out drops a cupcake with frosting, green sprinkles, and a cherry on top.

"Now that's a midnight snack!" thinks Freddie.

Swish! Boom! Bang! More cakes pop out of the machine and roll onto a conveyor belt.

"Wow!" says Freddie. "Just look at all these treats! They pop out of this machine faster than I can eat them. My imagination is really remarkably delicious sometimes!"

Soon Freddie is feeling full. Maybe his imagination is a little much! He feels his imagination taking over.

"I'd like a circus in the backyard, one that only I can see," he says.

"Honk! Hey, Freddie. Welcome to the circus!"

It is a silly clown with green hair, and a bright red nose. He is driving a funny little car. With him are other clowns, a princess with a crown, and a seal balancing balls on his nose.

"Come and join us. We're more fun than a barrel of monkeys!" say the clowns.

And they run around the yard, acting silly, as only clowns can do. The princess dances. The seal throws the balls up in the air and catches them on his nose.

After a while, Freddie announces, "Thanks for letting me be in your circus. Now I'd like to have a show of my own. You can be in it, too, if you like!"

And as soon as he says this, he finds himself on TV on his own TV show. He sings, and dances, and juggles, and balances balls on his own nose. He even does tricks that no one's ever seen before. The circus seals pick up Freddie and toss him up in the air.

Freddie's cat, Jingles, hops on top of the TV. Freddie sings Jingles a little song. Jingles purrs along to the music.

"Oh, anyone can be a TV star," Freddie says at last. "I think I'm ready to have another adventure. Lucky for me I have such a remarkable imagination. I wonder what I should do next?"

Freddie thinks about his sister Lucy, who has a new flashlight he has been admiring. But now that he has such a great imagination, a plain old flashlight doesn't sound like much fun.

"I know," he says, "I'll use the flashlight to create some magic beams for walking."

Suddenly Lucy is in his dream, along with his brother Sam, and their Dad.

Lucy shines the flashlight into a big mirror. Sam reflects the beams of light from the flashlight onto another mirror. Dad watches as Freddie walks in the air on the magic beams of light.

"Now that's a remarkable imagination, Freddie," says Dad.

"Walking on beams of light gets boring pretty fast," thinks Freddie. "I'd have more fun sledding."

Before he even turns over in his sleep, Freddie finds himself sliding down a snowy hill on a bright red sled. The sled glides smoother than any sled anyone could ever imagine. He passes by a boy and girl having a snowball fight at a snow fort.

"Wow, I'm imagining other people having fun, too," thinks Freddie.

"You have a remarkable imagination," they both say to Freddie. "But do you remember what night this is?"

Freddie thinks for a moment.

"Why, it's Christmas Eve," he says. "I imagine I should be helping Santa."

"Ho! Ho! Ho!" calls a strangely familiar voice.

"Santa!" calls Freddie.

"Come on, Freddie!" calls Santa.

Freddie climbs aboard Santa's magic sleigh. With a wink from the jolly old elf, they are high above the rooftops behind eight tiny reindeer.

Freddie peeks at the big bag Santa has tucked in the back of the sleigh.

"Are those the toys?" asks Freddie.

"They certainly are," says Santa. "Everything any boy or girl could imagine."

Santa is right. Inside the bag are all the things Freddie had imagined — gold doubloons, a treasure map, a rocket ship, clowns, cupcakes, some scary monsters, and even a flashlight.

Freddie rubs his eyes. It's Christmas! He had dreamed all night. Now he remembers the package. He jumps out of bed and races to the tree. Inside the box are mounds and mounds of tissue paper and another note.

The note says, "The gift of imagination will always be yours. Signed, S."

Freddie smiles. "Thank you, Santa," he says. Freddie looks toward the tree. "Hey! You guys get down from there!"

Just then, Mom comes into the room. "Who are you talking to?" she asks.

"Those silly guys playing with the decorations on the tree," says Freddie.

Mom looks at the tree. She doesn't see anyone.

"Freddie," says Mom, "you have a remarkable imagination."

"Thank you, I know. It was a gift from Santa," Freddie says with a wink.

Waiting
for Santa

Written by Pegeen Hopkins

Illustrated by Kathleen O'Malley

"Grandma, when will Santa be here?" little Sally asks as she crawls into bed. It is Christmas Eve. Everyone knows that on Christmas Eve, each minute is as long as a day.

"Santa will be here before you know it," Grandma says. "Let me tell you a story while we wait. When I was your age, I knew a young girl just like you. Her name was Lucy. She waited for Santa, too. As she helped her family decorate for Christmas, she asked her mother if Santa really lived on the North Pole, or right here in town."

"When the decorations were up, Lucy ran to find her grandfather. Surely he knew about Santa. He looked as old as Saint Nick, and knew everything besides. He had a bushy white beard, rosy cheeks, and when he laughed, his big round belly shook just like jelly. But his voice was the greatest. It was so deep, it rang out like a church bell.

"'Grandie, when will Santa get here?' Lucy asked. 'I've been waiting all day.'

"'That's just it,' her grandfather said. 'Santa only comes when you least expect him. That's the way all great things arrive.'"

"Was he right?" Sally asks Grandma.

"You'll see," Grandma answers. "Lucy joined her mother in the bedroom where they put on their best clothes for the party.

"'Mama,' Lucy said, 'Grandie knows so much. Don't you think he looks just like Santa? And Santa IS supposed to know everything. Grandie knows in a snap if I've been bad, even if he has been out.'

"Lucy's mother sighed. 'He is a special man, but do you really think he could be THE Santa Claus?'"

"Later that afternoon, Lucy and her family sat around the fire to sing Christmas carols. The singing stopped short when a loud thud came from the chimney.

"'What was that?' Lucy asked. 'I hear Santa! He's coming right now!' She ran out to the yard. But when she looked up on the roof, the roof was empty. Lucy trudged back inside.

"'Do you think,' said Lucy's grandfather, 'that Santa would come down a chimney filled with smoke and fire?'

"'You're right,' she replied."

"When the guests arrived and the party began, Lucy wondered how the other guests could be so patient. Weren't they thinking about Santa's arrival too?

"'It's getting late, Grandie,' she said. 'Maybe Santa is stuck in an ice storm and can't make it. Or one of his reindeer is sick and can't fly.'

"'Remember, my dear, you have to have faith,' said her grandfather. 'Be patient. There is no use in trying to figure him out. I think he wants to keep his comings and goings a secret.'"

"With that, Lucy's grandfather walked away. She watched him talk cheerfully to everyone in the room. Soon, Lucy forgot about waiting for Santa. She joined the rest of the party and the fun.

"After the night's last song, Lucy's grandfather hugged her and wished her a Merry Christmas. Only then did she realize it was close to midnight.

"'Grandie,' she said, 'the time flew by when I wasn't thinking about Santa. I had more fun, too.'

"Lucy's grandfather just smiled."

"Did the girl go to sleep without looking to see if Santa had come?" Sally asks.

"Not exactly," Grandma replies.

"As the last guests said goodnight, Lucy peeked at the Christmas tree, hoping new presents would be there. All she saw were the gifts her family had put there.

"'Time for bed,' Lucy's mother called. 'If you don't go to sleep now, Santa may never come.'

"Her father carried her up to bed. And before they reached her room, Lucy was fast asleep."

"Then, during the night, Lucy thought she heard sleigh bells jingling in the distance. Far off she heard a hearty 'Ho! Ho! Ho!' The voice was so familiar. Grandie? Lucy thought, half asleep. No, it couldn't be."

As she finishes her story, Grandma looks down at Sally. She has drifted off to sleep. Wishing her happy dreams, Grandma pulls up her covers and turns out the light. She walks downstairs to place a welcome wreath on the mantle for Santa. She thinks about herself all those years ago when she was the little girl in the story.

She looks at the wreath over the fireplace and remembers her Grandie, the gentleman with the shining eyes and an unmistakable voice. Could he really be Santa?

"It's possible," she says.

Joy to the World

Written by Sarah Toast

Illustrated by Linda Howard

Christmas will soon be here! The littlest herald angels trumpet the arrival of the best time of the year. It is the season when the littlest angels in heaven get to play with the children of the world as they prepare for Christmas. These littlest angels can't be seen or heard by children—not quite anyway.

Glad music and song fills the heavens as the littlest angels toot their trumpets, strum their harps, and play their drums. They make the heavens ring with joy and merriment!

Even the stars twinkle brighter. Children who look up into the heavens at this time of year can see the special brightness of the stars twinkling in the skies.

If the children stand very still and listen, they may hear the faint music of the littlest angels' celebration. The angels parade through the clouds, tooting their horns and ringing their bells. The music sounds like a music box being opened way up in heaven.

In a cozy home in a little town like many other towns, a mother and father have lit a fire in the fireplace. They are sitting down together to watch Jennifer and her little brother Jeff set up the Nativity scene.

Jennifer carefully arranges the Holy Family in the stable, with the infant Jesus lying on his back in the manger.

"I'm ready for the Wise Men now, Jeffie," she says to her brother. Jeff takes the Wise Men and their camels out of the box and hands them to Jennifer one by one.

Suddenly, a little angel begins to hover over their Nativity scene.

"Jeff, do you see what I see?" asks Jennifer with her eyes open wide.

"Yes, Jenny. The star above the stable is twinkling!" says Jeff.

"And I hear the whisper of an angel's wings," says Jennifer.

Mom and Dad smile and remember when they heard an angel's wings fluttering.

On the other side of town, James and Sally are taking the neighbor children, Jill and Robby, to see the department store windows on Main Street. The younger children are excited to see the windows decorated for Christmas.

"Look at Mary and Baby Jesus in the manger!" says Robby excitedly.

"And look at how that little angel's wings go up and down so gently," says Jill. They almost look real!

As the four children gaze at the window, one of heaven's littlest angels swoops down and hovers over the group.

"I think I hear the rustling of an angel's wings!" says Sally.

"And the halos over the heads of Mary and Baby Jesus are shining!" says James.

"The angel's halo is shining, too!" says Sally. Jill and Robby see it too.

"What a wonderful Christmas scene," says Jill as she points to the nativity.

Six little friends have gathered for their weekly play group. It is at Billy's house this time, when everyone is ready for Christmas.

"Let's make music and play Christmas songs!" says Billy. He plays the guitar while Tim and Susie beat on their drums. Josh plays the xylophone. Bitsy and Daniel begin to sing with tiny voices.

Every other time the play group has played music together, their music has sounded more like noise than a song. But today two little angels are visiting them. The angels bless the children with musical ability for a brief moment. When they finish their favorite Christmas song, the children, and the little angels, laugh with glee.

"We made beautiful music!" says Susie.

"And look up at the tree!" says Tim.

The children turn to look at the Christmas tree. They are amazed to see that the star on top is now twinkling and shining.

"Did our music do that?" they wonder.

Judy, Ron, and Stevie are making a really big snowman in the park.

"Here, Judy," says Ron. "We'll lift you up so you can put a carrot on the snowman's head to give him a nose."

Judy laughs. "This nose is really big!"

"I want to find out what a giant snowball tastes like," says Joe.

Two little angels watch the children playing just as Matthew and Emma throw themselves backward in the snow.

"You made a good snow angel," says Emma. "I'm going to try again." They laugh as they move their arms and legs in the snow.

The real angels laugh to see the children making snow angels on the ground. "Not bad," they think as they look at each other and smile.

The children stop for a moment to look at their snowman. Did the snowman wiggle his carrot nose?

They continue to play all day without ever feeling cold in their fingers or toes.

For weeks, the children in the Christmas choir have been practicing. Now it's time for the pageant.

As soon as the children begin to sing, the last little angel flies down and hovers above them. Of course, the children give their best performance ever, because they have been touched by the magic of Christmas!

Christmas Gifts

Written by Suzanne Lieurance

Illustrated by Deborah Colvin Borgo

It was Christmas Eve in the barnyard. Seven ordinary animals had just settled down for the night. It was just another ordinary night — or so they thought.

The hour of midnight drew near. Silent snow fell gently to the ground. And then something quite amazing happened. These seven ordinary animals, in this simple barn, became seven special animals, if only for this one night.

"What has happened?" asked the young sheep. "Baa! Baa! I can talk."

"Me, too!" said the dog. "Ruff! Ruff!"

"Moo-oo! Listen to me!" said the little calf.

"What's going on?" asked the surprised donkey. "Hee-haw!"

The cow wasn't surprised. "It's midnight," she said. "And it's Christmas Eve."

"What does that mean?" asked the sheep.

"I'll tell you a story," said the cow, "about the very first Christmas. Then you will understand."

All the animals in the barn gathered to hear the cow's story.

"Long, long ago, one special night," began the cow, "Baby Jesus was born in an ordinary stable, in an ordinary town called Bethlehem. This was the first Christmas."

"Was the stable like this barn?" the dog asked.

"Yes," said the cow, "almost exactly like it."

"With animals in the stable, just like us?" asked the young calf.

"Yes," said the cow, "with animals just like us. Let me explain.

"Before Baby Jesus was born, his mother, Mary, and her husband, Joseph, had to travel through the countryside to the town of Bethlehem. Their trip took many days. They traveled up and down steep hills. To make things easier for Mary, an ordinary donkey carried her on his back on this long trip and Joseph led the way."

"A donkey, just like me?" asked the donkey.

"Yes, a donkey just like you," said the cow.

"Finally, Mary and Joseph arrived in Bethlehem. But there was nowhere for them to sleep. They had to go to a stable and sleep with the animals. The donkey carried Mary safely to that stable."

"So it was an ordinary donkey who gave Baby Jesus a precious and unique gift, even before he was born, by carrying Mary safely to Bethlehem.

"Later that evening, inside the simple stable, Mary gave birth to a special baby named Jesus.

"The stable was cold. Luckily, in the stable lived a handsome sheep with very soft, beautiful wool."

"A sheep, like me?" asked the little sheep.

"Yes, just like you and your mother," answered the cow. "And this sheep's soft, beautiful wool was made into a very special blanket. The sheep offered this blanket, her unique and most precious gift, to the baby. Mary wrapped Baby Jesus in this special, soft, woolly blanket. It would keep the baby snug and safe during his stay in the stable."

"After their long journey, and the birth of the baby, Mary and Joseph were too tired for lullabies. They needed something to lull the baby to sleep. But what? Mary and Joseph were lucky to find a gentle dove living high in the rafters of the stable."

"A dove, just like me?" asked the dove.

"Just like you," said the cow. "And each night her soft cooing soothed the animals in the barn so they could enjoy a good night's sleep. That night the gentle dove began to coo very softly. This cooing quickly lulled Baby Jesus to sleep, as he lay covered with the sheep's special, soft, woolly blanket.

"But the baby still didn't have everything he needed, even with these most precious and unique Christmas gifts."

"Since Baby Jesus was so special, someone was needed to keep watch over him and his family. A brave dog lived in the stable. And though he was an ordinary dog, he was a very special watchdog."

"Just like me!" said the dog.

"Yes, just like you," said the cow. "All night, this brave dog stood watch at the door to the stable. No harm would come to Baby Jesus as long as he was around. The dog was glad to offer this precious and unique gift, and protect the baby from danger.

"All the animals in the stable gathered around Baby Jesus to adore him. Covered with a special blanket, lulled to sleep by the gentle cooing of the dove, the baby still needed some place very special to sleep."

"His mother could not hold him in her arms all night. So Mary needed a comfortable bed for her child. The ordinary cow came forward and offered the manger, her most precious and unique gift, so the baby would have a safe and soft place to rest his sweet head."

"An ordinary cow, just like you and me, Mom?" asked the young calf.

"Yes, just like you and me, dear," said the cow. "Mary and Joseph lined the manger with hay and tucked him under the soft woolen blanket.

"That night, something else happened that was special," continued the cow. "A bright star began to shine in the sky."

The animals were puzzled again.

"Where did the star come from?" asked the young calf.

"The star was a gift from God to announce to the world that a special baby had been born. It was the largest star in the sky. It shone over the earth to lead travelers from far and near to the Baby Jesus. In fact, the star was so bright, the stable glowed as the dog stood watch, with the cow and the donkey nearby.

"So you see," said the cow, "it was on a special night, in a simple stable like this one, that ordinary animals became special animals because of the unique and most precious Christmas gifts each of them offered Baby Jesus."

"It was a donkey, like me, who carried the baby's mother safely on his back," said the donkey.

"And a sheep, like me, gave her special woolen blanket," said the young sheep.

"Only a dove, like me, could have lulled the baby to sleep," cooed the dove.

"And it took a brave dog to keep watch over them all," said the dog, "just like me. Ruff! Ruff!"

"Yes, everyone has a unique and most special gift to give at Christmas," said the cow. "That's why animals like us are given this special gift of speech each Christmas Eve at midnight. So we might tell our children about those very first Christmas gifts given by ordinary animals."

The animals gathered at the door to the stable.
Suddenly they saw a bright star in the sky.

"Look! It's the same star!" said the young donkey.

"Yes," said the cow. "A special star, to always
remind us of that special night the most special
baby was born."

Christmas Angel

Written by Mary Rowitz

Illustrated by Laura Rader

Annie, the littlest Christmas angel, was very excited. Her first Christmas was just weeks away.

"If you keep jumping up and down, your wings will fall off," said Laura, a bigger angel. "Christmas is fun, but we have work to do."

"I don't mind," Annie said. "I want to help."

"Maybe you should just watch us," said Theresa, a bigger angel herself.

"Watch?" Annie cried. "But I want to help you, too." She took a wreath and ribbon from Laura. "Just because I'm little doesn't mean I can't help," Annie said.

Annie took the wreath and ribbon to a quiet corner. "How hard can it be?" Annie wondered.

A kitten angel held the ribbon as she unwound it and turned in circles. She became a little dizzy, but she didn't mind. The bigger angels were wrong. This was fun, not work.

"See? Just because I'm little doesn't mean I can't...help! HELP! I'm all tied up in a knot!"

Annie looked at the ribbon tied around her waist. "I look like a wreath. What if the bigger angels hang me on the front door?"

The bigger angels untied the littlest angel. "Let's see if we can keep you out of trouble," Theresa said. "Let's make cookies."

"How hard can that be?" Annie wondered. "I'm an expert at making cookies," Annie said. But she was really just an expert at eating them. She put eggs, butter, and flour in a bowl. Then she sat on the edge of the bowl and mixed the batter. This was fun, not work.

"Mmm. Like I've said, just because I'm little doesn't mean I can't...help! HELP! I've fallen into the bowl and I can't get out!"

The bigger angels lifted the littlest Christmas angel out of the bowl.

"Keeping you out of trouble is trouble itself," Laura said, giggling. "Let's see if you can help us wrap presents."

"How hard can that be?" Annie wondered. She cut a piece of paper. Then she cut a piece of ribbon. Before she folded the paper over the box, she peeked inside. This was fun, not work.

"See? Just because I'm little doesn't mean I can't...help! HELP! Now I've fallen into the box and I can't get out!" Annie rattled the green tissue paper over and over again.

The bigger angels lifted Annie out of the box.

"All right noisy one, why don't you help us hang some stockings...quietly," Theresa said.

"How hard could it be?" Annie wondered. She pushed a hook into the mantel of the fireplace. Then she hung a stocking onto each hook. This was fun, not work.

"Like I've said, just because I'm little doesn't mean I can't...help! HELP!" Annie fell off the mantel and became stuck on a hook! She spun in circles in midair. Annie hoped she wouldn't be stuck on the fireplace until Christmas!

The bigger angels found the littlest Christmas angel and let her down from the fireplace.

"Come sing with us," Laura said.

"But I want to play the harp just like you do," Annie said.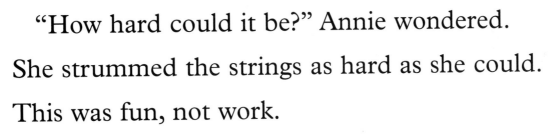

"Okay," Theresa said. "We'll sing and you can play the harp."

"How hard could it be?" Annie wondered. She strummed the strings as hard as she could. This was fun, not work.

"See? Just because I'm little doesn't mean I can't...help! HELP! I've broken a string!"

The bigger angels stopped singing.

"Well, I could sing now," Annie said.

The bigger angels agreed that Annie should do something she had done before: painting.

"Just be sure to paint the paper, not your dress," Laura said.

"Of course," Annie thought. "How hard could that be?"

She put the jar of paint fa-a-r-r-r away from her elbow so she wouldn't spill it. Then she carefully spread the paint onto the paper.

Painting was fun, not work. "Just because I'm little doesn't mean I can't...help! HELP! What a mess!" Annie spilled paint on her dress!

The bigger angels helped the littlest angel change into a clean dress.

"Let's do something that won't make a mess," Theresa said. "Let's hang ornaments."

"How hard could that be?" Annie wondered. She removed the ornaments from the box. Annie wrapped her arms around the ornaments and hung them on the tree branches. This was fun, not work.

"See? Just because I'm little doesn't mean I can't...help! HELP! My dress is stuck on one of the branches, and I can't get down!"

After the bigger angels got the littlest Christmas angel down, Laura suggested that they take a break from their work.

"Let's make a snowman," she said.

"How hard could that be?" Annie wondered. She grabbed a fistful of snow and rolled it into a ball. This was the most fun of all!

"Like I've said, just because I'm little doesn't mean I can't...help! HELP! I've rolled myself up into the snowball!"

Annie flew down the hill and—splat!—crashed into the snowman. His head fell to the ground. So did his belly.

Finally, it was Christmas morning. As the bigger angels sang carols by the tree, they noticed the branches moving. The littlest Christmas angel was climbing the tree!

"Now this is work," Annie said. "But you can't have a Christmas tree without an angel on top," Annie said, raising her arms up high.

The littlest Christmas angel was so happy that, for the first time, her halo began to glow.

The Night Before Christmas

Written by Clement C. Moore

Illustrated by Tom Newsom

'Twas the night before Christmas,

when all through the house

Not a creature was stirring,

not even a mouse.

The stockings were hung

by the chimney with care,

In hopes that St. Nicholas

soon would be there.

The children were nestled

all snug in their beds,

While visions of sugarplums

danced in their heads;

And Mama in her kerchief,

and I in my cap,

Had just settled our brains

for a long winter's nap,

When out on the lawn

there arose such a clatter,

I sprang from my bed

to see what was the matter.

Away to the window

I flew like a flash,

Tore open the shutters

and threw up the sash.

The moon on the breast

of the new-fallen snow

Gave a luster of midday

to objects below.

When what to my wondering eyes

should appear

But a miniature sleigh

and eight tiny reindeer,

With a little old driver,

so lively and quick,

I knew in a moment

it must be St. Nick!

More rapid than eagles

his coursers they came,

And he whistled and shouted

and called them by name:

"Now, Dasher! Now, Dancer!

Now, Prancer and Vixen!

On, Comet! On, Cupid!

On, Donder and Blitzen!

To the top of the porch!

To the top of the wall!

Now dash away! Dash away!

Dash away, all!"

As dry leaves that before

the wild hurricane fly,

When they meet with an obstacle,

mount to the sky,

So up to the housetop

the coursers they flew,

With a sleigh full of toys—

and St. Nicholas, too.

And then, in a twinkling,

I heard on the roof

The prancing and pawing

of each little hoof.

As I drew in my head

and was turning around,

Down the chimney St. Nicholas

came with a bound.

He was dressed all in fur,

from his head to his foot,

And his clothes were all tarnished

with ashes and soot;

A bundle of toys

he had flung on his back,

And he looked like a peddler

just opening his pack.

His eyes, how they twinkled!

His dimples, how merry!

His cheeks were like roses,

his nose like a cherry!

His droll little mouth

was drawn up like a bow,

And the beard on his chin was

as white as the snow.

The stump of a pipe

he held tight in his teeth,

And the smoke,

it encircled his head like a wreath.

He had a broad face

and a little round belly

That shook, when he laughed,

like a bowl full of jelly.

He was chubby and plump,

a right jolly old elf,

And I laughed when I saw him,

in spite of myself.

A wink of his eye

and a twist of his head

Soon gave me to know

I had nothing to dread.

He spoke not a word,

but went straight to his work,

And filled all the stockings,

then turned with a jerk,

And laying a finger

aside of his nose,

And giving a nod,

up the chimney he rose.

He sprang to his sleigh,

to his team gave a whistle,

And away they all flew

like the down of a thistle.

But I heard him exclaim,

ere he drove out of sight,

"Happy Christmas to all,

and to all a good night!"

Santa's Gift

Written by Lisa Harkrader

Illustrated by Kathy Couri

Santa tiptoed across the rug. It was Christmas Eve, Santa's favorite night of the year. He slipped a skinny present under Cat's Christmas tree.

"Ho-ho-ho," chuckled Santa. "Cat will love this fishing pole." Santa's elves had worked extra hard to make Cat's gift extra special.

"My elves make every gift special," said Santa. "How can I show them how much I appreciate everything they do?" Santa stroked his beard. His eyes twinkled. "I know!" he said. "I'll give them a special gift, too."

But what would be special enough? Santa looked at Cat's gift. A fishing pole was perfect for Cat.

"But not perfect for my elves," said Santa. "Where can they fish at the North Pole?"

Santa shook his head and climbed into his sleigh. "I'll have to think of something else to give them," he said.

Santa visited Rooster next. Rooster's present was small. "But it's every bit as special as Cat's fishing pole," said Santa, "thanks to my elves."

Rooster's gift was an alarm clock. The elves had worked hard building the clock. It was beautiful, and it kept perfect time.

Santa looked at Rooster's gift. An alarm clock was the perfect gift for Rooster. Would it be the perfect gift for the elves?

"No," said Santa. "My elves are already very prompt. I'm afraid an alarm clock wouldn't do them any good."

Santa sighed. "I'll have to think of something else," he said.

Santa's next stop was Bear's den. Santa couldn't wait to give Bear his gift. "A cuddly teddy bear for a cuddly big bear," said Santa.

Santa remembered how his elves had carefully stitched the teddy bear. They picked just the right buttons for the teddy bear's eyes and just the right ribbon for the teddy bear's bow tie. They wanted it to be the perfect gift for Bear.

"And it is perfect for Bear," said Santa. "But not perfect for my elves. They sleep with their own teddy bears every night."

Santa scratched his head. "I'll have to think of something else," he said, as he tiptoed out the door past a sleeping Bear.

It was Santa's favorite night of the year, but he
was starting to feel very sad. He couldn't think of a
special gift for his elves.

Santa cheered up when he reached Squirrel's tree house. He knew Squirrel would love her gift.

"A nutcracker," said Santa. He could imagine Squirrel's delight when she opened it. "She'll be so happy her tail will flutter," he said.

The nutcracker was the perfect gift for Squirrel.

"But not the perfect gift for my elves," said Santa. "They don't need to crack nuts. They can eat all the nuts they want in the North Pole Candy Kitchen."

Santa trudged back to his sleigh. The night was half over and he still didn't have a gift for his elves. "I'll have to think of something soon," he said.

Santa visited Zebra's house next. Zebra's gift was extra special.

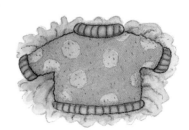

"A polka-dot sweater," said Santa. "My elves knitted every stitch by hand."

Santa imagined how thrilled Zebra would be. "He'll be so happy he'll click his hooves together," Santa said.

A polka-dot sweater was the perfect gift for Zebra.

"But not perfect for the elves," said Santa. "They live at the North Pole. They have all kinds of sweaters—red and green, purple and blue, stripes and checks, polka-dots and squiggles."

Santa heaved his bag over his shoulder. "I'll have to think of something else," he said. "But what?"

The next house belonged to Skunk. Santa gave Skunk the smallest present of all. But it was also the most special gift of all.

"A lovely bottle of perfume," said Santa.

Santa knew Skunk wanted perfume more than anything else. She loved to smell nice when she went dancing.

He could almost see her smile as she opened it. "She'll be so happy her nose will twitch," he said.

Santa brightened. Perfume was a very special gift. None of the elves had perfume.

Then he sighed and shook his head. "When would they use perfume?" he said. "My elves never go dancing. They never leave the North Pole."

Santa was very sad when he left Skunk's house. He hung his head and headed to the next house. "What if I don't think of something special enough?" he asked.

Next Santa visited Fish. He had a very special gift for her.

"A snorkeling set," said Santa.

Santa imagined how excited Fish would be when she opened it. "She'll be so happy her fins will flap," he said.

The snorkeling set was the perfect gift for Fish.

"But not for my elves," said Santa. "They live at the North Pole. They can't go snorkeling in ice."

Santa sighed. He was very sad. He'd been trying all night to think of a gift for the elves, but nothing was special enough. As he turned to leave, he took one last long look at the gift he'd given Fish.

Santa stroked his whiskers. "My elves can't go snorkeling in ice and snow," he murmured. "No, they certainly can't."

The next stop was Rabbit's house. Santa slid a funny shaped package under Rabbit's tree.

Santa's eyes twinkled. "I'd love to be here when Rabbit opens his gift," said Santa. "He'll be so happy his ears will quiver."

Rabbit's gift was a pogo stick. The elves had thought of it.

They wanted to give Rabbit something to keep his hopping from being humdrum.

The pogo stick was perfect for Rabbit.

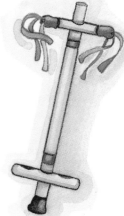

"Not exactly perfect for my elves, though," said Santa. He leaped into his sleigh. "But I think I know what is perfect. Something to keep them from feeling humdrum."

Now, Santa just needed to work out the details.

Santa's last stop was Ant's house. Santa left a big, bulky gift in Ant's parlor.

"I wish I could see her face when she opens it," said Santa. "She'll be so happy she'll dance on all six feet."

Ant's gift was a picnic basket and picnic blanket. The elves had carefully woven the basket and packed it with Ant's favorite foods: fried chicken and fruit salad and chocolate cake.

"Ant works hard all year long," said Santa. "She deserves to take a leisurely picnic once in a while."

The basket was perfect for Ant.

"But the gift for my elves will be even more perfect," said Santa.

He tossed his empty bag into the sleigh and grabbed the reins. "Now I know exactly what to give them," he said.

When the sleigh pulled into the North Pole, the elves gathered to greet Santa. But he wasn't inside.

"Oh, heavens!" cried Mrs. Claus. "Where could he be?"

Inside the sleigh was a large gift. The elves untied the bow and out jumped Santa, wearing a Hawaiian shirt and shorts.

"Find your suitcases and grab your teddy bears," said Santa.

The elves looked at each other, puzzled.

"This is my gift to you," said Santa. "To thank you for all your hard work, I'm taking you on a long vacation. Merry Christmas!"

Jingle Bells

Written by Sarah Toast

Illustrated by Kathleen O'Malley

Andrew and his sister Arabella live in town. Andrew works in Mr. Ward's store, and Arabella teaches school. Their family—Mother, Father, Ned, Sue, and Grandpa—all live on the farm where Andrew and Arabella grew up.

It's Christmas Eve. Andrew and Arabella have been planning a wonderful Christmas surprise for their family. They ask Mr. Ward if they can borrow Nelly and the sleigh.

"Why, certainly!" says Mr. Ward. "It is my Christmas gift to you."

Andrew walks to Mr. Ward's stable. He puts a leather strap with jingle bells on Nelly's tail and ties a bright red ribbon around her neck.

Andrew hitches up the sleigh. He tosses in a warm blanket and guides Nelly out the gate. He and Nelly pass a watchful snowman as they glide toward town to get Arabella. The sun is just starting to set in the early evening sky.

The bells on Nelly's tail jingle and jangle with the rhythm of her prancing steps. Andrew whistles "Jingle Bells" as the sleigh glides along the snowy path.

Arabella has had to work today, too. But now she waits anxiously for Andrew at the boarding house where she lives. Her spirits are bright with happiness at the thought of their Christmas surprise.

The lights are coming on in the houses in town as Nelly pulls Andrew down the center of Main Street. Andrew thinks about how far it is to the farm, where his family is gathered together for Christmas. Even aunts, uncles, and cousins are visiting at the farm for the holiday.

At the end of the street, Andrew passes a group of Christmas carolers. They make their way from house to house singing songs of Christmas joy. Nelly's jingling bells add cheerful music to the carolers' songs. Andrew smiles as he passes the singers. He slows down as he comes to the boarding house where Arabella stays.

Andrew stops outside the boarding house. He hitches Nelly to the post.

Arabella puts on her hat and gloves and is already at the door before Andrew can even ring the bell.

"Andrew, do you think they know we're coming?" Arabella asks.

"No," he says. "They know that we worked today. They wouldn't expect us tonight."

Nelly swishes her tail, jingling the bells, as Andrew helps Arabella up into the sleigh.

"I'm so glad we already sent our presents," says Arabella with a twinkle. "That will surely make them think we couldn't come."

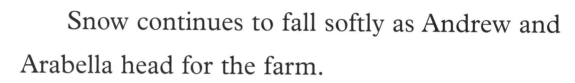

Snow continues to fall softly as Andrew and Arabella head for the farm.

"I'm so eager to see Mother and Father and Grandpa again," says Andrew.

"And little Ned and Sue," says Arabella. "Do you think they'll like the nice presents we sent them?"

"We'll get to see when they open them, won't we?" Andrew replies. "With any luck, we'll be home before they even wake up!"

The sky is getting darker as night falls, but the starlight and moonlight on the snow make the night bright and sparkly.

Andrew and Arabella talk of Christmases when they were little as Nelly pulls them home. They sing favorite Christmas songs and laugh when the jingling bells don't match their song.

Around midnight, clouds blow across the bright face of the moon. The stars are hidden as well. Andrew and Arabella are not even halfway home yet, and they are nearing the deep woods.

Among the trees, it is difficult to see the road. But Nelly is strong, and seems to know the way.

"I knew I'd seen Nelly before," says Andrew. "She's from the horse farm next to Mother and Father's farm!"

It isn't long before the clouds disappear.
The moonlight reflects brightly off the snow.
But the late hour and the rhythm of the jingling
bells are making Arabella and Andrew sleepy.

"Andrew, how about if I take a turn at the
reins so you can take a nap?" suggests Arabella.

"Are you sure?" asks Andrew.

"Yes," says Arabella. "I have been looking
forward to driving Nelly."

Soon only the sound of Nelly's bells breaks
the deep silence. Arabella marvels at the purple
shadows cast on the snow in the moonlight. She
is filled with awe by the haloed stars crowding
the Christmas Eve sky.

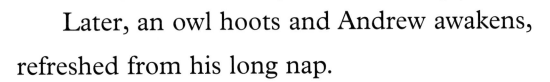

Later, an owl hoots and Andrew awakens, refreshed from his long nap.

"Your turn to sleep, Arabella," says Andrew. He takes the reins and Arabella naps.

Arabella awakens as the sky brightens to greet Christmas day.

"We're almost there, Andrew!" she exclaims when she sees the familiar shape of the family farmhouse ahead. "I can't wait to surprise the family on Christmas morning!"

It isn't long before they turn onto the road that leads up to their gate. Already there is a light on in the kitchen. Mother is up making hot chocolate and coffee.

Sleepy faces peer out of the windows as Nelly brings the sleigh right up to the door. Mother runs out to hug Arabella and Andrew.

"My goodness! We didn't think you would be home for Christmas this year!" says Mother.

The windows fly open, and voices young and old shout, "Merry Christmas, Andrew! Merry Christmas, Arabella!"

What a merry Christmas surprise!

The Christmas Kitten

Written by Lara Jackson

Illustrated by Anastasia Mitchell

It was Christmas Eve, and Santa still needed a kitten for one little girl who had been especially good. "Where will I ever find a real kitten?" Santa asked.

Suddenly, Santa heard a sad little meow. He turned around and saw a kitten in the snow. "Little kitten, are you lost?"

"No, I don't have a home," the kitten cried.

"I've got the perfect place for you," Santa said. And he put the happy kitten in his sack full of presents. "Don't go anywhere, little kitten."

Just then, a tiny mouse ran past. Without thinking, the kitten quickly ran after the mouse.

When Santa returned, the kitten was gone! He looked everywhere, but he couldn't find the little kitten!

"Little kitten, where are you?" Santa called out as he scratched his whiskers.

Santa listened for the kitten's meows. But all he heard was the blowing wind. He searched through all of his toys, but no kitten!

Suddenly he saw a patch of tiny paw prints in the snow. "Hmm, maybe these prints will lead me to the kitten," Santa thought to himself. So he followed the prints to the stable.

When he got to the stable, Santa looked inside. But he didn't see the kitten anywhere!

"Kitten! Kitten! Santa is here to take you to your new home!" he called.

Just then, Santa heard a rustling noise. He walked toward the noise, and it got louder and louder. But when he turned the corner he only saw Comet eating hay.

"Hello! Care for some hay?" Comet asked.

"Have you seen a little kitten in the stable?" Santa asked Comet.

Comet just shook his head and continued eating the hay.

Santa had to find the kitten before midnight! So he went to the toy workshop where the elves were busy making the last gifts. He heard the shrill whistle of the workshop train. Santa waved at the conductor to stop the train.

"Stop! Stop! Mr. Conductor, have you seen any kittens?" Santa shouted.

"No kittens today, only Christmas presents," Mr. Conductor answered.

"Thanks, Mr. Conductor," Santa said as he waved the train along.

"I'll keep my eye out for a kitten!" Mr. Conductor yelled back to Santa.

Santa slowly walked up to the second floor of the workshop. The elves were working so hard that they didn't notice when Santa walked into the room.

"Has anyone seen a kitten?" Santa asked.

One elf, named Danny, dropped his tools and looked at Santa. "A kitten? No. Sorry, Santa," answered Danny. "Nothing but toys here, Santa," he added.

Then Jack-in-the-Box popped up and yelled, "I saw a kitten! She went that way!"

"Thank you, Jack-in-the-Box!" Santa yelled as he followed Jack's pointing finger out the door.

Santa ran to the main house and looked everywhere, calling, "Kitten! Where are you?"

Santa walked over to the mantle. "Maybe she climbed into one of the stockings," Santa thought to himself.

Santa looked in each stocking, turning them all inside out. He reached for the last stocking. He thought he felt something small and soft, like a kitten! "Kitten, are you in this stocking?" he asked.

But when he looked inside, all he found was a little doll. Santa was disappointed again. "Where could the kitten be? Maybe she's under the Christmas tree."

He walked over to the giant Christmas tree and looked under and over everything! He even shook all of the packages under the tree to check if the kitten was in one of them.

"Where are you, little kitten?" Santa began to pace. He walked around and around the tree.

Then Santa saw something under the tree that he missed before. Could it be the kitten? "Come on out, little kitten," he said. He reached for the small object.

Woo-woo! Santa found a red, shiny fire truck and its siren sounded in his hand. Santa would not give up his search!

"I've checked everywhere and there is still no sign of that kitten!" Santa exclaimed.

Suddenly a loud rumble came from the home of the toy soldiers. The door popped open and out marched the toy soldiers! The toys wanted to look for the kitten, too.

"We will help you, Santa!" they shouted.

Santa looked at the toy soldiers' house and saw something brown and fuzzy! "Hmm, maybe the kitten is hiding in here," Santa said.

But all he found was a big teddy bear!

Santa slowly walked back to his sleigh. "I have to leave now," Santa said sadly.

"No, Santa, don't go yet! The kitten is near!" The toys in the sack shouted.

"What? Where is she?" Santa asked.

"Maybe you should look in your sack one more time, Santa," the toys yelled.

Santa looked through his sack again. He heard a little meow coming from a french horn. As he turned the french horn upside down, the Christmas Kitten jumped out!

"There you are! I've been looking all over for you, little kitten!" Santa exclaimed.

Off they flew through the air!

"That's your new home!" Santa shouted to the kitten as he pointed to the house below.

Santa landed on top of the house. He took the kitten down the chimney with him.

"Hang on, little kitten!" Santa said.

When they landed inside the house, Santa said, "Welcome to your new home!"

"Oh thank you, Santa!" the kitten purred.

"Merry Christmas, Christmas Kitten!"

Christmas Socks

Written by Sarah Toast

Illustrated by Debbie Pinkney

It is Christmas Eve. Santa and his elves have been working hard all year to make toys and dolls for children all over the world.

Santa's big bag is packed to overflowing with drums and bears, dolls and balls—all sorts of things to delight good little children on Christmas morning.

"But, Santa," says an elf. "How does your bag hold a toy for every child?"

"Ho, ho, ho!" laughs Santa kindly. "When I leave gifts under the Christmas trees, magic fills my bag up again!"

"That's amazing, Santa!" says the elf.

Just then, Mrs. Claus dashes out of the house. "My dear, don't forget the candy for all the Christmas stockings!"

"Thank you very much!" says Santa. He climbs into his sleigh. His sleigh is so full that Mrs. Claus can barely see Santa!

In one house below, David and Molly are fast asleep. They are dreaming a wonderful dream of Santa and his reindeer flying through the sky to their house.

David and Molly had written a letter to Santa with their secret Christmas wish in it. It took them a long time to write the letter. When they had finished, they showed their letter to their mother.

"Now that your letter is done, I'll help you bake Christmas cookies. Then you can leave your letter for Santa next to the cookies so he will be sure to see," said Mom.

After the cookies came out of the oven, Molly and David decorated them. Before the two children went to bed that night, they piled cookies on a big plate. Next to it they put a glass of milk and their letter.

"Santa won't be able to miss it," said David.

Now the two children are sound asleep in their beds as Santa's journey brings him closer to their house with each stop he makes.

At last Santa arrives at the rooftop of David and Molly's house. The reindeer land so softly on the roof that there's not even a bump, just the faint jingle of jingle bells. Snug in their beds in the bedroom below, David and Molly dream on about their special request.

"The chimney looks a little snug," Santa says. Santa has to fit down the chimney with his big bag of toys and a special something tucked in his jacket. But with a deep breath and a little Christmas magic, he slides down the chimney with hardly a scrape, big belly, big pack of toys, and all.

Santa looks around. "What a nice tree. I bet David and Molly helped to decorate it."

Santa puts some presents underneath the tree for David and Molly. Then he thinks to himself, "Goodness, I've gone many miles already tonight, and I'm getting a bit hungry! Can't stop yet, though. I've got more to do here before I can have a bit of a rest."

Santa goes over to the mantle where the stockings are hung. "Now, where are Mrs. Claus's candies?" he thinks. Santa reaches inside his pack for the candies.

Santa fills all the stockings with candy canes, peppermint sticks, cinnamon balls, and other Christmas goodies. Even Mom and Dad get Mrs. Claus's candy treats.

At last, Santa pats the special something tucked in his jacket and says, "Now for a treat!"

Santa looks around and sees the cookies and milk on the small table.

"Ah!" says Santa. "I knew it! Molly and David have left out a big plate of Christmas cookies for me. Just what I need to finish my deliveries to all the other children on my list."

But before Santa takes a bite, he goes to the kitchen and brings back a saucer. Then he pours some of the milk into the saucer and sets it on the floor. He unbuttons his jacket and says, "Come on out and have some milk!"

Santa leans back and enjoys the cookies. He eats almost all the Christmas cookies on the plate and drinks the rest of his milk.

Then Santa picks up the letter from Molly and David.

Santa's eyes twinkle. "I already know what this says," he chuckles. "I knew it as soon as they wrote the letter!"

"To Santa," the letter begins. "We have been good all year. We have helped our Mom and Dad a lot. We took care of Mrs. Jasper's cat when she was away. We really liked the cat. So, we read books about how to take care of a pet."

"Will you please bring us a cat for Christmas," continues the letter. "We will take good care of it and love it." The letter is signed, "From your friends, Molly and David."

Santa picks up the empty saucer and takes it to the kitchen. When he returns, he says, "Did you enjoy your milk, Socks?"

Socks answers with a contented purr. Then she settles down to dream sweet cat dreams about a nice boy and girl to play with.

Santa gives a merry wave with his mittens as he bounds up the chimney.

David and Molly wake up Christmas morning and hurry downstairs.

"Hooray! Santa brought us a cat, just like we wanted!" David and Molly look at each other and say, "I think we should name our new kitty Socks."

The Perfect Tree

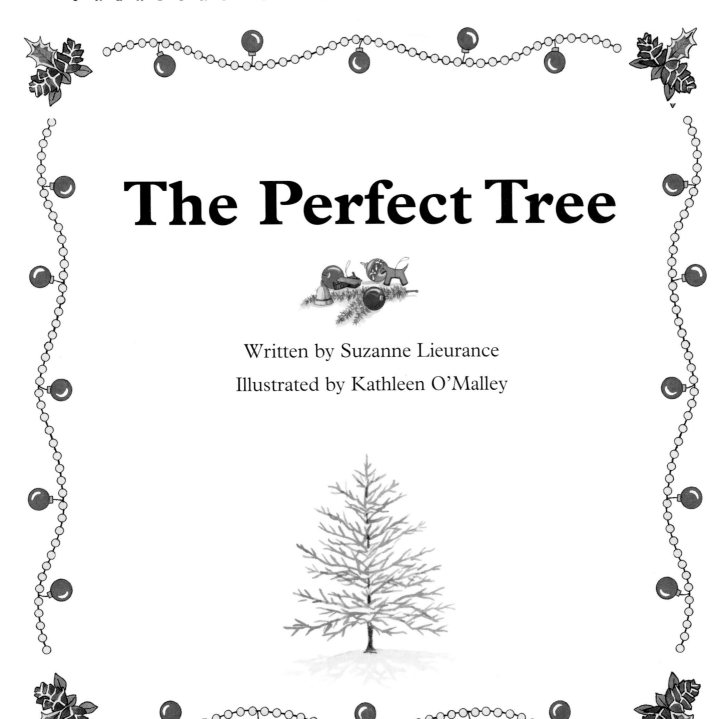

Written by Suzanne Lieurance

Illustrated by Kathleen O'Malley

"The big pine trees are the prettiest trees," the little pine says to himself.

It is Christmastime in the forest and all the trees are excited about the season. Their thick branches are covered with blankets of snow—all the branches except for the little pine's, that is.

"Who would want such a little tree with such thin branches?" he says.

"Don't worry," says the biggest spruce in the forest, "someone will think you're special."

"All of you trees are special," chirps a little bird, sitting on a snowy bough.

But the little pine isn't so sure. His branches droop a little.

"Hey, wait for me!" Sarah calls. "I want to pick the tree this year!"

Her brother David scoops up some soft snow and makes a snowball.

"Not if I get there first," he shouts. He throws the snowball at a lamppost.

Dad and Mom follow as they all start out on a snowy walk to the forest.

"Remember," says Mom, "it can't be too broad, or it won't fit through the door."

"And it can't be too tall," says David, "or it will scrape the ceiling."

"We'll know the perfect tree when we see it," says Sarah.

Soon the family arrives at the forest. The trees can't wait to see which tree will be picked.

The children race right past the giant spruce trees. They stop at the little pine.

"This one!" decides Sarah.

"Yeah! It's perfect!" says David.

The children dance around the little pine.

"Hmm," says Mom, "not too broad."

"And it won't scrape the ceiling," says Sarah.

"Looks just right to me," says Dad.

"See," says the biggest spruce, "someone thinks you're special already."

"They can't mean me," says the little pine. "Look at my thin little branches."

Dad examines the tree closely. "The trunk isn't very broad. It'll be easy to cut," he says.

"Be careful," says Mom.

"I'll be very careful," says Dad. "I won't hurt our tree a bit."

Dad begins to saw the bottom of the little pine's trunk.

"What beautiful, straight branches," says Mom. "Such a lovely little tree."

"See? They don't think your branches are too skinny," says the largest spruce. "They think you're special."

The little pine still drooped. "They think I'm special now. But wait till they get me home."

Once the little pine is cut, Dad carefully wraps it with twine.

"The twine makes sure the branches won't bend and break off," he tells the children.

Sarah and Dad lead the way home with their new tree tied securely onto the sled.

"Where will we put the tree?" asks David.

"In front of the window," says Mom, "so everyone can see our perfect little tree."

"The decorations will be so beautiful," Sarah says. "Our tree will be the best one ever!"

"I hope the decorations look right on my skinny little branches," the little pine thinks. "I don't want to disappoint my new family."

At home, Dad and David make a tree stand for the little pine. Dad puts a bowl of water at the bottom of the tree's trunk.

"What's that for?" asks David.

"To give the tree a drink," says Dad. "We need to take care of our perfect little tree."

Sarah and Mom watch as Dad and David get everything ready.

"Look," says Sarah. "People can see our tree from both front windows."

"You're right," says Mom. "Everyone will get to admire our special tree."

"Oh no," thought the little pine. "Everyone will see how silly the decorations look on me!"

Mom gets up from her chair. "Time to start decorating," she says.

"What can we do?" Sarah and David ask.

"Start with these," says Mom, scooting some boxes near the tree. Inside the box are bright ornaments of all shapes, sizes, and colors.

"Ooh, they are so shiny," says Sarah.

"Some of them were Grandma's favorite ornaments," says Mom.

"What a lucky tree," says David, "to wear such special ornaments."

"I'll place the angel on the top," says Dad.

The little pine is worried the angel will not be able to balance on his thin top branches.

David and Sarah hang shiny ornaments on the little pine's branches until the boxes are empty. Mom wraps the tree with garlands of red ribbon. The angel Dad placed atop the highest branch proudly watches over everything.

"Isn't it the most beautiful tree you have ever seen?" asks Sarah.

"It certainly is," says Dad.

"How lucky we were to find such a special tree," says David.

The little pine perks up. "The family isn't disappointed after all. Maybe the big spruce trees were right."

The family admires their beautiful tree.

David glances out the window. "Look!" he says. "It's snowing."

"This is the perfect Christmas," says Mom.

The little pine stands proud and straight. "The spruce trees were right," he thinks. "Being special doesn't always mean being the biggest or the most beautiful. In the forest, I thought that I was a scrawny little pine. But now I know that I truly am special."

Christmas Songs

Over the River and Through the Woods

O-ver the ri-ver and through the woods to Grandmo-ther's house we go.   The

horse knows the way   to car-ry the sleigh through the white and drift-ed   snow.

O-ver the ri-ver and through the woods, Oh, how   the wind   does   blow!   It

stings   the toes   and bites   the nose   As   o - ver the ground we go!

Here We Come A-Caroling

Oh, here we come a-

car - o - ling a - mong the leaves so green;

Here we come a - wan - d'ring so fair to be

seen: Love and joy come to

you, And to you glad ti - dings, too; And God

bless you and send you a hap - py New

Year, And God send you a hap - py New

Year!

2. We are not daily beggars
     That beg from door to door;
   We are the neighbors' children
     Whom you have seen before.
   Love and joy come to you,
     And to you glad tidings, too;
   And God bless you and send you a
       happy New Year,
     And God send you a happy New Year.

3. We have got a little purse
     Of stretching leather skin;
   We want a little of your money
     to line it well within,
   Love and joy come to you,
     And to you glad tidings, too;
   And God bless you and send you a
       happy New Year,
     And God send you a happy New Year.

4. Bring us out your table,
     And spread it with a cloth.
   Bring us out your moldy cheese,
     And some of your Christmas loaf.
   Love and joy come to you,
     And to you glad tidings, too;
   And God bless you and send you a
       happy New Year,
     And God send you a happy New Year.

5. God bless the master of this house,
     Likewise the mistress, too;
   And all the little children
     That round the table go.
   Love and joy come to you,
     And to you glad tidings, too;
   And God bless you and send you a
       happy New Year,
     And God send you a happy New Year.

Mary Had a Baby

Mar-y had a Ba-by, Oh, Lord,—— Mar-y had a Ba-by,

Oh, my— Lord. Mar-y had a Ba-by, Oh, Lord,—— The

peo - ple keep a com - ing and the train—— done gone.

2. What did she name Him,
  Oh, Lord;
She called Him Jesus,
  Oh, my Lord;
Where was He born?
  Oh, Lord;
The people keep a-coming and the
  train done gone.

3. Born in a stable,
  Oh, Lord;
Where did they lay Him?
  Oh, my Lord;
Laid Him in a manger,
  Oh, Lord;
The people keep a-coming and the
  train done gone.

Gather Around the Christmas Tree

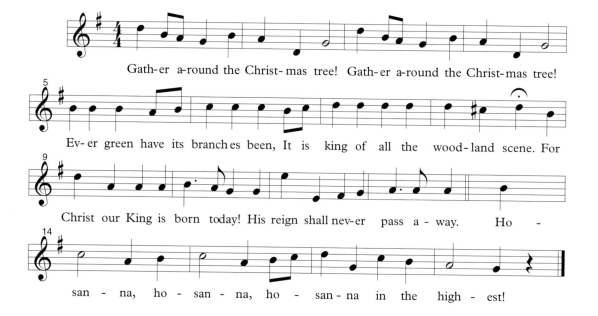

Gath-er a-round the Christ-mas tree! Gath-er a-round the Christ-mas tree!

Ev-er green have its branch-es been, It is king of all the wood-land scene. For

Christ our King is born today! His reign shall nev-er pass a-way. Ho -

san - na, ho - san - na, ho - san - na in the high - est!

2. Gather round the Christmas tree!
    Gather round the Christmas tree!
Once the pride of the mountainside,
    Now cut down to grace our Christmastide.
For Christ from heaven to earth came down,
    To gain through death a nobler crown.
Hosanna, hosanna, hosanna in the highest!

3. Gather round the Christmas tree!
    Gather round the Christmas tree!
Every bough has a burden now,
    They are gifts of love for us, we trow.
For Christ is born, His love to show,
    And give good gifts to men below.
Hosanna, hosanna, hosanna in the highest!

Infant Holy
Infant Lowly

In-fant ho-ly, in-fant low-ly, For His bed a cat-tle stall; Ox-en low-ing, lit-tle know-ing, Christ the babe is Lord of all. Swift are wing-ing an-gels sing-ing, Now-ells ring-ing, tid-ings bring-ing, Christ the babe is Lord of all, Christ the babe is Lord of all.

2. Flocks were sleeping, shepherds keeping,
   Vigil till the morning new,
Saw the glory, heard the story,
   Tidings of a gospel true.
Thus rejoicing, free from sorrow,
   Praises voicing, greet the morrow,
Christ the babe was born for you,
   Christ the babe was born for you.

The Holly and the Ivy

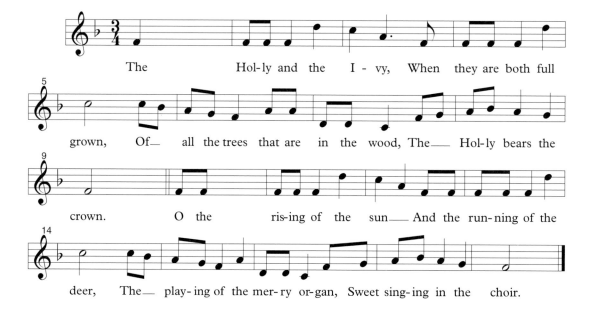

The Hol-ly and the I - vy, When they are both full grown, Of— all the trees that are in the wood, The— Hol-ly bears the crown. O the ris-ing of the sun— And the run-ning of the deer, The— play-ing of the mer-ry or-gan, Sweet sing-ing in the choir.

2. The Holly bears a blossom,
   As white as any flower;
   And Mary bore sweet Jesus Christ
   To be our sweet Savior.

   O the rising of the sun,
   And the running of the deer,
   The playing of the merry organ,
   Sweet singing in the choir.

3. The Holly bears a prickle,
   As sharp as any thorn;
   And Mary bore sweet Jesus Christ
   On Christmas day in the morn.

   O the rising of the sun,
   And the running of the deer,
   The playing of the merry organ,
   Sweet singing in the choir.

4. The Holly bears a berry,
   As red as any blood;
   And Mary bore sweet Jesus Christ
   To do poor sinners good.

   O the rising of the sun,
   And the running of the deer,
   The playing of the merry organ,
   Sweet singing in the choir.

5. The Holly bears a bark
   As bitter as any gall;
   And Mary bore sweet Jesus Christ
   For to redeem us all.

   O the rising of the sun,
   And the running of the deer,
   The playing of the merry organ,
   Sweet singing in the choir.

Toyland

Toy - land! Toy - land!

Lit — tle girl and boy land. While you

dwell with - in it You are ev - er hap - py

then. Child - hood's joy -

land, Mys — tic mer - ry Toy - land!

Once you pass its bor - ders you can nev - er re -

turn a - gain.

Angels From the Realms of Glory

An - gels from the realms of glo - ry,

Wing your flight o'er all the earth; Ye, who sang cre -

a - tion's sto - ry, Now pro - claim Mes - si - ah's birth:

Come and wor - ship! Come and wor - ship! Wor - ship Christ the

new - born King!

2.Shepherds, in the field abiding,
　Watching over your flocks by night,
　God with man is now residing,
　Yonder shines the infant light.
　Come and worship!
　　Come and worship!
　Worship Christ, the newborn King!

3. Sages, leave your contemplations,
　Brighter visions beam afar.
　Seek the great Desire of nations
　Ye have seen His natal star.
　Come and worship!
　　Come and worship!
　Worship Christ, the newborn King!

4. All creation, join in praising,
　God, the Father, Spirit, Son,
　Evermore your voices raising,
　To the eternal Three in One.
　Come and worship!
　　Come and worship!
　Worship Christ, the newborn King!

A Child Now Is Born in Bethlehem

A child now is born in Beth - le -
hem, Beth - le - hem. Re - joice you
now, Je - ru - sa - lem. Al - le - lu - ja, Al -
le lu - ja!

2. Three Kings came from Sheba
   By the star, by the star.
   With incense, gold, and myrrh from afar,
   Alleluia, Alleluia!

We Three Kings

We three kings of O- ri- ent are, Bear- ing gifts we tra- verse a- far,

Field and foun- tain, moor and moun - tain, Fol- low- ing yon- der star.

O_____ star of won- der, star of night, Star with roy- al beau- ty bright,

West- ward lead- ing, still pro- ceed- ing Guide us to Thy per- fect light._____

2. Born a King on Bethlehem's plain,
   Gold I bring to crown Him again,
King forever, ceasing never,
   Over us all to reign.
O star of wonder, star of night,
   Star with royal beauty bright,
Westward leading, still proceeding,
   Guide us to Thy perfect light.

3. Frankincense to offer have I,
   Incense owns a Deity nigh.
   Prayer and praising, all men raising,
   Worship Him, God most high.
   O star of wonder, star of night,
   Star with royal beauty bright,
   Westward leading, still proceeding,
   Guide us to Thy perfect light.

4. Myrrh is mine, its bitter perfume,
   Breathes a life of gathering gloom;
   Sorrowing, sighing, bleeding, dying,
   Sealed in the stone-cold tomb.
   O star of wonder, star of night,
   Star with royal beauty bright,
   Westward leading, still proceeding,
   Guide us to Thy perfect light.

5. Glorious now behold Him arise,
   King and God and sacrifice,
   Alleluia, alleluia;
   Earth to the heav'ns replies.
   O star of wonder, star of night,
   Star with royal beauty bright,
   Westward leading, still proceeding,
   Guide us to Thy perfect light.

Away in a Manger

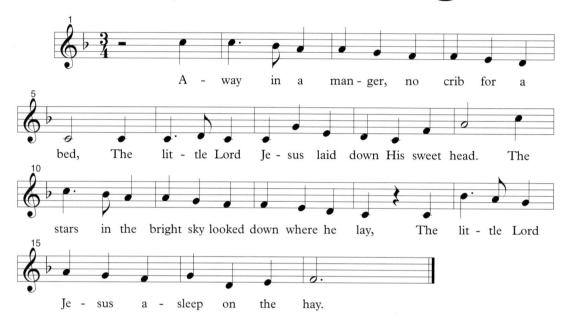

A - way in a man - ger, no crib for a bed, The lit - tle Lord Je - sus laid down His sweet head. The stars in the bright sky looked down where he lay, The lit - tle Lord Je - sus a - sleep on the hay.

2. The cattle are lowing, the poor baby wakes,
   But little Lord Jesus, no crying He makes.
   I love thee, Lord Jesus, look down from the sky,
   And stay by my cradle to watch lullaby.

3. Be near me, Lord Jesus, I ask thee to stay,
   Close by me forever, and love me, I pray.
   Bless all the dear children in thy tender care,
   And fit us for heaven, to live with thee there.

Fum, Fum, Fum

Vein-te cin-co de di-ciem-bre, Fum, fum, fum. Vein-te cin-co de di-ciem-bre,

On December twen-ty-five, Fum, fum, fum. On December twenty-five,

Fum, fum, fum. Na-ci-do por nuestro amor el Niño Dios el Niño Dios. Hoy de

Fum, fum, fum. Born is He for love of us, the Son of God, the Son of God. Born is

la Virgen Maria En es-ta no-che tan fri-a. Fum, fum, fum.

He of Virgin Mary On this night so cold and drea-ry. Fum, fum, fum.

Hark the Herald Angels Sing

2. Christ, by highest heaven adored,
   Christ, the everlasting Lord,
Late in time behold Him come,
   Offspring of a virgin's womb.
Veiled in flesh the Godhead see;
   Hail, the incarnate Deity,
Pleased as Man with man to dwell,
   Jesus, our Immanuel!
Hark! the herald angels sing,
   "Glory to the newborn King."

3. Hail, the heaven-born Prince of Peace!
   Hail, the Sun of Righteousness!
Light and life to all he brings,
   Risen with healing in his wings.
Mild he lays his glory by,
   Born that man no more may die,
Born to raise the sons of earth,
   Born to give them second birth.
Hark! the herald angels sing,
   "Glory to the newborn King."

God Rest Ye Merry Gentlemen

God rest ye, mer - ry gen - tle - men let noth - ing you dis - may, Re - mem - ber Christ our Sa - viour was born on Christ - mas day, To save us all from Sa - tan's power when we were gone a - stray. O - ti - dings of com - fort and joy, com-fort and joy, O - ti - dings of com - fort and joy.

2. From God our Heavenly Father,
    A blessed angel came,
And unto certain shepherds,
    Brought tidings of the same,
How in that Bethlehem was born,
    The Son of God by name.
O tidings of comfort and joy,
    comfort and joy,
O tidings of comfort and joy!

3. 'Fear not,' then said the angel,
    'Let nothing you affright,
This day is born a Savior,
    Of a pure virgin bright,
To free all those who trust in Him
    From Satan's power and might.'
O tidings of comfort and joy,
    comfort and joy,
O tidings of comfort and joy!

4. The shepherds at those tidings
    Rejoiced much in mind
And left their flocks a-feeding,
    In tempest, storm, and wind,
And went to Bethlehem straightway,
    This blessed babe to find.
O tidings of comfort and joy,
    comfort and joy,
O tidings of comfort and joy!

5. And when they came to Bethlehem,
    Where our dear Savior lay,
They found Him in a manger,
    Where oxen feed on hay;
His mother Mary kneeling down,
    Unto the Lord did pray.
O tidings of comfort and joy,
    comfort and joy,
O tidings of comfort and joy!

6. Now to the Lord sing praises,
    All you within this place,
And with true love and brotherhood,
    Each other now embrace;
This holy tide of Christmas,
    All others doth deface.
O tidings of comfort and joy,
    comfort and joy,
O tidings of comfort and joy!

Rocking

Lit-tle Je-sus, sweet-ly—sleep, do not—stir; We will—lend a—

coat of— fur, We will rock you, rock you, rock you, We will rock you, rock you, rock you:

See the fur to keep you warm, Snug-ly— round your— ti-ny— form.

2. Mary's little baby, sleep, sweetly sleep,
   Sleep in comfort, slumber deep;
   We will rock you, rock you, rock you,
   We will rock you, rock you, rock you:
   We will serve you all we can,
   Darling, darling little man.

Bring a Torch

Bring a torch,—Jean-ette, Is- a-bel- la, Bring a torch,—come swift- ly and run.

Christ is born, tell the folks of the vil-lage, Je-sus is sleep-ing in His cradle. Ah, ah,

Beau-ti-ful is the Moth-er,　Ah,　ah,　Beau-ti-ful　is her　Son.

2. It is wrong when the child is sleeping,
   It is wrong to talk so loud.
   Silence, all, as you gather around,
   Lest your noise should waken Jesus.
   Hush! hush! see how fast He slumbers,
   Hush! see how fast He sleeps!

3. Softly to the little stable,
   Softly for a moment come.
   Look and see how charming is Jesus,
   How He is white and His cheeks are rosy!
   Hush! hush! see how the child is sleeping,
   Hush! see how He smiles in dreams!

Up on the Housetop

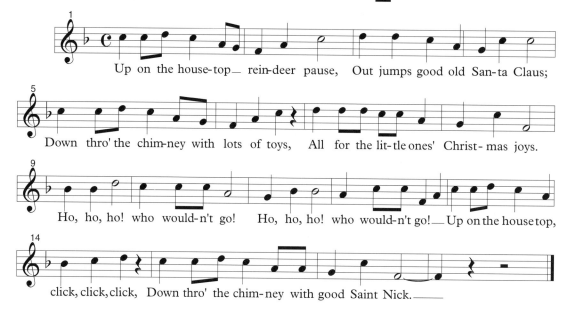

Up on the house-top— rein-deer pause, Out jumps good old San-ta Claus;

Down thro' the chim-ney with lots of toys, All for the lit-tle ones' Christ-mas joys.

Ho, ho, ho! who would-n't go! Ho, ho, ho! who would-n't go!— Up on the house top,

click, click, click, Down thro' the chim-ney with good Saint Nick.——

2. First comes the stocking of little Nell;
   Oh, dear Santa, fill it well;
   Give her a dolly that laughs and cries,
   One that can open and shut its eyes.
   Ho! Ho! Ho! Who wouldn't go?
   Ho! Ho! Ho! Who wouldn't go?
   Up on the housetop,
   click, click, click!
   Down through the chimney with
   good Saint Nick.

3. Next comes the stocking of little Bill;
   Oh, just see that glorious fill!
   Here is a hammer and lots of tacks,
   Whistle and ball and a set of jacks.
   Ho! Ho! Ho! Who wouldn't go?
   Ho! Ho! Ho! Who wouldn't go?
   Up on the housetop,
   click, click, click!
   Down through the chimney with
   good Saint Nick.

Angels We Have Heard on High

An - gels we have heard on high,

Sweet - ly sing - ing o'er the plains. And the moun - tains

in re-ply Ec - ho - ing their joy - ous strains:

Glo_____

ria_____ in ex - cel - sis de - o.

Glo_____

ria_____ in ex - cel - sis de_____ -

o.

2. Shepherds, why this jubilee?
    Why these songs of happy cheer?
   What great brightness did you see?
    What glad tidings did you hear?
   Gloria in excelsis deo.
     Gloria in excelsis deo.

3. Come to Bethlehem and see,
    Him whose birth the angels sing.
   Come adore on bended knee,
    Christ, the Lord, the newborn King.
   Gloria in excelsis deo.
     Gloria in excelsis deo.

4. See Him in a manger laid,
    Whom the angels praise above.
   Mary, Joseph, lend your aid,
    While we raise our hearts in love.
   Gloria in excelsis deo.
     Gloria in excelsis deo.

Joy to the World

Joy to the world! The Lord is come; Let earth re-ceive her King;——— Let every——— heart——— pre-pare— Him—room——And heav'n and nature—sing And— heav'n and na-ture— sing; And—heav'n— and heav'n——and na-ture sing.———

2. Joy to the world! the Savior reigns!
   Let men their songs employ,
While fields and floods, rocks, hills, and plains,
   Repeat the sounding joy,
Repeat the sounding joy,
   Repeat, repeat the sounding joy.

3. No more let sins and sorrow grow,
   Nor thorns infest the grounds;
He comes to make His blessings flow,
   Far as the curse is found,
Far as the curse is found,
   Far as, far as the curse is found.

4. He rules the world with truth and grace,
   And makes the nations prove,
The glories of His righteousness,
   And wonders of His love,
And wonders, of His love,
   And wonders, wonders of His love.

O Come All Ye Faithful

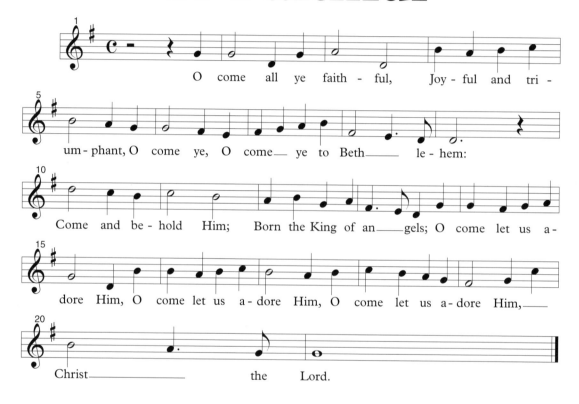

O come all ye faith - ful, Joy - ful and tri - um - phant, O come ye, O come — ye to Beth — le - hem: Come and be - hold Him; Born the King of an — gels; O come let us a - dore Him, O come let us a - dore Him, O come let us a - dore Him, — Christ — the Lord.

2. Sing choir of angels, sing in exultation,
    O sing, all ye citizens of heaven above!
  Glory to God, in the highest;
    O come, let us adore Him,
    O come, let us adore Him,
    O come, let us adore Him,
    Christ the Lord.

3. See how the shepherds, summoned to His cradle,
    Leaving their flocks, draw nigh to gaze;
  We too would thither bend our joyful footsteps;
    O come, let us adore Him,
    O come, let us adore Him,
    O come, let us adore Him,
    Christ the Lord.

4. Child, for us sinners poor and in the manger,
    We would embrace thee, with love and awe;
  Who would not love thee, loving us so dearly?
    O come, let us adore Him,
    O come, let us adore Him,
    O come, let us adore Him,
    Christ the Lord.

5. Yea, Lord, we greet thee, born this happy
      morning,
    Jesus, to thee be all glory giv'n;
  Word of the Father now in flesh appearing;
    O come, let us adore Him,
    O come, let us adore Him,
    O come, let us adore Him,
    Christ the Lord.

See Amid the Winter's Snow

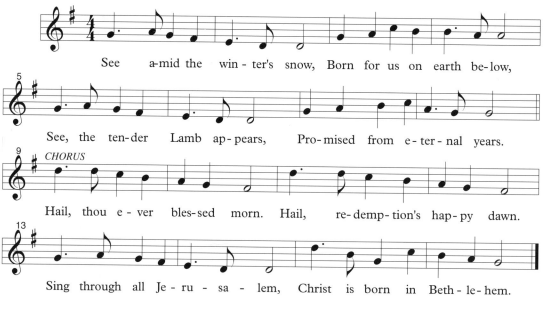

See   a-mid the   win-ter's snow, Born for us on earth be-low,

See, the ten-der   Lamb ap-pears,   Pro-mised from e-ter-nal years.

CHORUS

Hail, thou e-ver   bles-sed morn. Hail,   re-demp-tion's hap-py   dawn.

Sing through all Je-ru-sa-lem,   Christ is born in   Beth-le-hem.

2. Lo, within a manger lies
     He who built the starry skies;
   He, who throned in height sublime,
     Sits amid the cherubim,
   Hail thou ever blessed morn.
     Hail, redemption's happy dawn.
   Sing through all Jerusalem,
     Christ is born in Bethlehem.

3. Say, ye holy shepherds, say,
     What your joyful news today;
   Wherefore have ye left your sheep,
     On the lonely mountain steep?
   Hail thou ever blessed morn.
     Hail, redemption's happy dawn.
   Sing through all Jerusalem,
     Christ is born in Bethlehem.

4. 'As we watched at dead of night,
     Lo, we saw a wondrous light;
   Angels singing peace on earth,
     Told us of the Savior's birth.'
   Hail thou ever blessed morn.
     Hail, redemption's happy dawn.
   Sing through all Jerusalem,
     Christ is born in Bethlehem.

5. Sacred infant, all divine,
     What a tender love was thine,
   Thus to come from highest bliss
     Down to such a world as this.
   Hail thou ever blessed morn.
     Hail, redemption's happy dawn.
   Sing through all Jerusalem,
     Christ is born in Bethlehem.

6. Teach, O teach us, holy child,
     By Thy face so meek and mild,
   Teach us to resemble Thee,
     In Thy sweet humility.
   Hail thou ever blessed morn.
     Hail, redemption's happy dawn.
   Sing through all Jerusalem,
     Christ is born in Bethlehem.

What Child Is This

2. This, this is Christ the King,
   Whom shepherds guard and angels sing;
   Haste, haste, to bring Him laud, the Babe,
   The Son of Mary.

3. So bring Him incense, gold, and myrrh,
   Come, peasant, King, to own Him.
   The King of Kings salvation brings,
   Let loving hearts enthrone Him.

4. This, this is Christ the King,
   Whom shepherds guard and angels sing;
   Haste, haste, to bring Him laud, the Babe,
   The Son of Mary.

O Little Town of Bethlehem

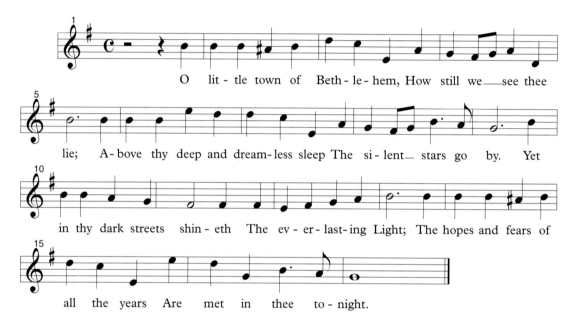

O lit - tle town of Beth - le - hem, How still we see thee lie; A - bove thy deep and dream - less sleep The si - lent stars go by. Yet in thy dark streets shin - eth The ev - er - last - ing Light; The hopes and fears of all the years Are met in thee to - night.

2. For Christ is born of Mary,
   And gathered all above,
   While mortals sleep, the angels keep
   Their watch of wond'ring love.
   O morning stars, together,
   Proclaim the holy birth,
   And praises sing to God the King,
   And peace to men on earth!

3. How silently, how silently,
   The wondrous gift is giv'n!
   So God imparts to human hearts
   The blessings of His heav'n.
   No ear may hear His coming,
   But in this world of sin,
   Where meek souls will receive Him still,
   The dear Christ enters in.

4. O holy child of Bethlehem,
   Descend on us, we pray;
   Cast out our sin and enter in;
   Be born in us today!
   We hear the Christmas angels
   The great glad tidings tell;
   O come to us, abide in us,
   Our Lord Emmanuel!

It Came Upon a Midnight Clear

It came up-on a mid-night clear, that glorious song of

old, From angels bending near the earth To touch their harps of gold.

"Peace on earth goodwill to men From heav'n's all gracious King." The world in solemn

still - ness lay To hear the angels sing.

2. Still through the cloven skies they come,
   With peaceful wings unfurled,
   And still their heavenly music floats
   O'er all the weary world;
   Above its sad and lowly plains
   They bend on hovering wing,
   And ever o'er its Babel sounds,
   The blessed angels sing.

3. Yet with the woes of sin and strife
   The world hath suffered long,
   Beneath the angel-strain have rolled
   Two thousand years of wrong;
   And man, at war with man, hears not
   The love song which they bring:
   O hush the noise, ye men of strife,
   And hear the angels sing.

4. And ye, beneath life's crushing load,
   Whose forms are bending low,
   Who toil along the climbing way
   With painful steps and slow:
   Look now! for glad and golden hours
   Come swiftly on the wing;
   O rest beside the weary road,
   And hear the angels sing.

5. For lo! the days are hastening on,
   By prophet-bards foretold,
   When, with the ever-circling years,
   Shall come the Age of Gold;
   When peace shall over all the earth
   Its heavenly splendors fling,
   And all the world give back the song
   Which now the angels sing.

Merry Christmas!